THE WISDOM
OF THE ELDERS

THE WISDOM
OF THE ELDERS

ROBERT FLEMING

One World
Ballantine Books • *New York*

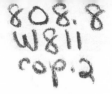

A One World Book
Published by Ballantine Books

Copyright © 1996 by Robert Fleming

First Edition: February 1996

10 9 8 7 6 5 4 3 2 1

This book is dedicated with love and respect to the elders who most influenced me with their wisdom: my great-grandmother, Ida Hollingshead; my grandfathers, Will Fleming and Allen C. Smith; and my grandmothers, Rose Smith and Mary Taylor.

CONTENTS

PREFACE

"Always listen to people who've lived with a sense of purpose and commitment to something bigger than themselves," said my grandfather, Allen C. Smith, a wise and generous Ohio farmer who aided hundreds of people during the Great Depression. "Anyone who has lived on this earth with a sense of mission for half a century or more is worth paying attention to. So be quiet and listen to what they have to say, it'll make the road ahead easier for you."

For some time now I've wanted to create a book that would honor the ancients of our race, the only unwilling immigrants to the New World. Despite being a captured people transported to a strange land, robbed of language, culture, and family ties, they continue to guide and inspire us with their courageous fight for freedom, human rights, and full citizenship.

Time and time again, our Elders refused to surrender to the tyranny of politics and the segregationist policies intended to demean their very humanity. Their pride in their race, their strength of will, and their persistence made me incredibly proud to be an African American.

These were people of great courage and stature. We need to learn from their example, for their words are as true for us today as they were when they were first written. And, in fact, *The Wisdom of the Elders* was designed to be a commentary on our times. As I researched it, I was struck by the political and social parallels between the eras of our esteemed Elders and our own. In many ways, not much has changed, except for the increasing subtlety and sophistication of the obstacles placed in our path.

There is a clear connection between the losses we faced in the nineteenth century post-Reconstruction period and the current Conservative backlash. After the Civil War, Blacks enjoyed ten good years of political and cultural progress during the Reconstruction Era, from 1865 to 1877. Because of the influence of leading Northern businessmen intent on punishing the South, a weak Congress passed the 14th Amendment, ensuring rights for Blacks. A major civil rights bill granting former slaves U.S. citizenship was narrowly passed in 1866. Suddenly, the former slave states found themselves confronted by legions of Black freedmen who organized themselves into a potent political force; they seized significant control in several Southern states.

This parallels the 1960s when much progress was made in defeating the old segregationist Jim Crow laws, in the teeth of ongoing opposition from whites. There was Alabama governor George Wallace's run for the presidency; Richard Nixon's and Spiro Agnew's law and order campaign of 1969; and Congress's increasing reluctance to guarantee Blacks protection from rampant police brutality and the fascist tactics of the FBI.

In the late 1860s and 1870s, similar Conservative forces

coalesced to resist the reforms of Reconstruction. White opposition never stopped working to reverse the gains made by their ex-slaves. In the late 1860s, they instituted the Black Codes, which essentially said: We will never accept you Blacks as anything but slaves.

The Reconstruction period officially ended in 1876 when candidate Rutherford B. Hayes made a deal with Southern interests to remove political safeguards for Blacks in the South. With the help of the Supreme Court, the door was opened for the political oppression of the segregationist Jim Crow laws.

The parallels to the present are strong: In the 1880s and 1890s, the Southern states rolled back the equalitarian laws in much the same way Congressional Conservatives in the 1990s are rolling back the gains of the Civil Rights Movement.

The irony is that we thought that integration would be the solution to all of our problems. True integration has not been achieved, however, and I doubt it will ever be. But maybe that's a good thing. Because a color-blind America would mean the end of Black American culture and society as we know it.

There was a time when Black neighborhoods were vibrant and solid, when they were fertile ground for family and community. All that changed when the idea of integration was introduced, and the newly mobile Black middle class fled the ghettos. Only the poor remained, and our African American community has never been the same.

The rumblings we hear from the ghettos now are the angry, frustrated cries of people who know they have been shunned and abandoned by the larger white society and, even more painfully, by their own people as well. Their fashions, their music, their sense of style may have been co-opted by mainstream America, but as a people, they will always be a side dish to the main entrée, and they know it. Today, every slum in this country is a challenge to the basic American belief in our essential goodness and generosity. But the challenges also offer us an opportunity to express these values.

After so many years of privilege, many white Americans are finding it very difficult to share power with all the minorities in this country. Conservatives are using the so-called "pathologies" of the urban poor as justification for their efforts to throw out all the gains made by Blacks in the 1960s and 1970s. The issues of race and class are again being injected into every crucial area of American life as a means of division and diversion from the very real economic and societal difficulties we all face. At the root of all this is the deep reluctance of many whites to abandon their myths of superiority and to commit themselves to racial justice and a sense of fairness. Because of their rejection of an America for all Americans regardless of race or creed, we find ourselves living in an atmosphere of increasing social turbulence and cultural mayhem.

The common view among many of those currently in power is: Everything will be fine again once Blacks and women are put back in their place. Recent Supreme Court rulings echo and re-echo those of the post-Reconstruction era, dismantling Federal affirmative action programs and blocking the restructuring of electoral districts to dilute the political clout of minority voters. They say that if existing Civil Rights laws are enforced, there should be no need for Federal involvement in "The Negro Question."

Still, *The Wisdom of the Elders* shows us that while we may be down, we're very far from being defeated! Our Elders faced much more serious battles and never surrendered. Neither will we. These pages hold the vision, the courage, the will, and the creative energy we need to keep moving forward.

As Frances Ellen Watkins Harper said in 1891:

"A government which can protect and defend its citizens from wrong and outrage and does not is vicious. A government which would do it and cannot is weak."

And as June Jordan said a hundred years later in 1987:

"We have been flexible, ingenious and innovative or we have perished. And we have not perished."

The Wisdom of the Elders blends the collective voices and thoughts of our greatest visionaries, teachers, and warriors in candid statements on many of the key issues of their time—and ours. You will see many of our Elders revealed in a wholly different light from their usual public personas. For example, we don't particularly think of Richard Pryor as a romantic. Yet there's tenderness and power in his 1986 thoughts on love.

"But there's intimacy. . . . To be that close. Or just touch someone's cheek. . . . And look in someone's eyes and know that you're looking at the truth."

Writer Richard Wright once called us "America's metaphor." He felt that the way the African American community is being viewed and treated at any point in our history reflects the social and political mood in the country as a whole.

In this book you will discover many metaphors, many images, many views. But every entry yields a gem of thought-provoking, race-proud wisdom. Every entry insists that we take an unflinching look in the mirror, both as individuals and as a community. As Toni Morrison said in 1975:

". . . Black people must be the only people who set out our criteria in criticism. White people can't do it for us. That's our responsibility and in some way we have to do it. I say you must always tell the truth. And I tell you that we are not weak people and we can stand it."

This is the challenge and the wonder of the voices assembled here. They ask tough questions. They demand creative and innovative answers. Take W. E. B. Du Bois's thought-provoking statement on parenthood in 1947:

"The mothers and fathers and the men and women of our race must often pause and ask: Is it worth while?
Ought children be born to us?
Have we a right to make human souls face what we face today?"

The answers to Du Bois's difficult questions can only come through contemplating our collective experiences, drawing from the vast richness of our cultural and political legacy. Distinguished historian John Henrik Clarke believes the current generation of African Americans is not fully aware of this legacy. His concerns inspired me to assemble the entries into these fourteen categories:

· Power and Politics   · Community
· Creativity and Culture   · Relationships
· Self-Esteem   · Black Women and Black Men
· Values   · A Living God
· Youth   · Race and Racism
· Education   · Freedom
· Family   · Strategies for Change

Following each Elder's entry, I've added a brief commentary called "Reflection," because the Elders mirror our times and issues, and because they also ask us to reflect upon these ideas—and ourselves. These essays look beyond the fragmentation, despair, and various plagues our communities face, to remind us of the hope, the healing power, and the special kind of clear-eyed, tell-it-like-it-is philosophy that has always shaped our view of ourselves and the world.

This book is meant to be used as a catalyst for real change—personal and collective. Since it was designed to stimulate discussion about our current choices as a community, there are ideas here that will probably make you mad. But they'll also make you think. And that's the whole point. *The Wisdom of the Elders* is about looking at ourselves, owning up to what we see, and growing from there. It's about asking ourselves what we're doing to improve the circumstances of our people. It's about asking ourselves who we are, and where we go from here.

Acknowledgments

The Wisdom of the Elders would not have been possible without the steadfast guidance and support of my editor, Cheryl D. Woodruff, who put in long hours at my side shaping and hand-polishing this book. Many thanks to Barbara Shor for her excellent line editing and to Gary Brozek for his invaluable assistance in helping this project cross the finish line. Much appreciation goes to Vanessa N. Quijano and Betsy Flagler for countless hours of manuscript typing under intense pressure.

THE WISDOM

OF THE ELDERS

Part 1

POWER
AND POLITICS

HISTORY REPEATS ITSELF

*Even in Congress, the white people, the dominant race, are begin-
ning to throw in our teeth that enough has been done for us, and we
must now take care of ourselves. I do not object to this. We are nu-
merous enough, and all we need is to be intelligent enough to take
care of ourselves. We are four millions, out of thirty millions who
inhabit this country and we have rights as well as privileges to
maintain and we must assert our manhood in their vindication.*

*. . . With this force as a political element, and as laborers, pro-
ducers and consumers, we are an element of strength and wealth too
powerful to be ignored by the American people. All we need is a just
appreciation of our own power and our own manhood. . . . I strike
out boldly, as if born in a desert, and looking for civilization. I am
groping about through this American forest of prejudice and pro-
scription, determined to find some form of civilization where all men
will be accepted for what they are worth. I demand nothing for our
race because they are black. Even the wrongs of two hundred years
I will overlook, although they entitle us to some consideration. Still,
I hope the future will present no necessity for frequent reference to
this matter.*

—P. B. S. Pinchback,[1] 1875

REFLECTION: Time doesn't always heal all wounds. Sometimes history repeats itself. Back in 1875, Pinchback saw America tell its newly freed Black citizens that it had exhausted its financial resources on our rehabilitation. Defying Washington, the Southern states moved to scale back all the gains we'd made since the Civil War. Prominent Blacks denounced President Grant for not caring enough about the still-oppressed Negro, while the response from many Northern whites was that too much had been done already.

In the late 1990s, countless social programs are getting the ax. The old battle cry to return to an oppressive past is being heard again. Some say enough has been done for us. According to one conservative congressman, it's time for us to get out of the wagon and push. The need for vigilance to ensure that reactionaries and racists do not succeed in creating a new Jim Crow code based on gender, class, and race has never been greater. We cannot allow ourselves to be forced back to what and where we were.

My time is now! History may repeat itself, but we can create a new and lasting resolution this time around.

BLACK PRIDE

*Black people are saying a very powerful, complex, yet simple thing:
"I am a man." The struggle of racism all along has been a struggle
to regain the essential manhood lost after the European expansion
into the broader world and the attempt to justify the slave trade.
This struggle has brought us to where we are now, standing on the
"black and beautiful" plateau. From this position Black people will
go into another stage, much higher and more meaningful for mankind. After reclaiming their own humanity, I think they will make
a contribution toward the reclamation of the humanity of man.
First, they will have to realize that in the kind of world we live in,
being black and beautiful means very little unless we are also black
and powerful. There is no way to succeed in the struggle against
racism without power. That is a part of our new reality and our
new mission.*

—*John Henrik Clarke*,[2] *1970*

REFLECTION: Today we possess the power of the vote. We earned this right with the blood and sacrifice of many of our people in a protracted struggle in both the North and South. And yet, many of us don't even register to vote. We bemoan the state of affairs in the nation, but when the time comes to take an active hand in shaping our destiny, we step back into the shadows.

This is why our voice in political matters is in danger of becoming a muffled whisper. It's important to take pride in who we are, but that pride must be matched with action. Know the issues, not just those that affect you but also those that affect your neighbor. Those who would do us harm recoil at the thought of an informed electorate holding them accountable to a new standard. We must exercise the power of self-determination at the ballot box.

Black pride and Black power are oppression's worst enemies. I will vote in my own best interests and in the interests of my community.

COLLECTIVE EFFORT

I did not get on that bus to get arrested; I got on the bus to go home. Getting arrested was one of the worst days in my life. It was not a happy experience. Since I have always been a strong believer in God, I knew that He was with me, and only He could get me through the next step.

I had no idea that history was being made. I was just tired of giving in. Somehow, I felt that what I did was right by standing up to that bus driver. I did not think about the consequences. I knew that I could have been lynched, manhandled, or beaten when the police came. I chose not to move. When I made that decision, I knew that I had the strength of my ancestors with me.

—Rosa Parks,[3] 1994

REFLECTION: On December 1, 1955, in Montgomery, Alabama, Rosa Parks decided she was too tired to move to the back of the bus. This quiet seamstress violated a Jim Crow law by refusing to give up her seat and was put in jail. During her arrest, she wondered if the "colored" community would rally around her and support her act of courage. Her prayers were answered! Her community backed her and organized a bus boycott that lasted 381 days. Not only did it spark the Civil Rights Movement, it pressured the Supreme Court to render a decision proclaiming that segregation on all public transportation was illegal.

We are an incredible people when we focus on a goal. We have enormous stamina and resilience. Across the nation today, a new agenda of fiscal expediency and social insensitivity is in place, imperiling the funds for many of the agencies supporting our most needy communities. The same persistence and organizational skills we exhibited in Montgomery must be used to meet this new menace. Monitor what is going on around you. Attend public hearings. Demand accountability.

The collective force of our community can sustain us through any crisis. Together, we are unstoppable.

POLITICS

What the black man needs is a country and surroundings in harmony with his color and with respect for his manhood. . . . Thousands of white people in this country are ever and anon advising the colored people to keep out of politics, but they do not advise themselves. If the Negro is a man in keeping with other men, why should he be less concerned about politics than any one else? . . . For the Negro to stay out of politics is to level himself with a horse or a cow, which is no politician, and the Negro who does it proclaims his inability to take part in political affairs. If the Negro is to be a man, full and complete, he must take part in everything that belongs to manhood. If he omits a single duty, responsibility, or privilege, to that extent he is limited and incomplete.

—Bishop Turner,[4] 1896

REFLECTION: In late summer 1995, a white TV commentator, analyzing the possible field of presidential candidates for the upcoming election, quickly ruled out General Colin Powell as a viable contender. He noted that white America is not ready for a Black or female president, but would tolerate a symbolic run for the White House by either one. It was his belief that any attempt by either party to seriously advance a presidential candidate who was Black or female would be tantamount to conceding the race before it had even begun. While Powell initially basked in the media spotlight of his book tour, those spotlights turned to searchlights as the hardball presidential politics began.

As African Americans, we cannot let others set the limits of our political involvement. We must be fearless and aggressive players in both the local and national political scene. From the statehouse to the White House, we must be active in shaping the politics of our nation.

Only a fool allows others to set his limits. From voting in elections to serving as an elected official—political participation is my right and my responsibility.

THE POWER OF THE BALLOT

It is unfair to expect a white administration to protect the Negro when the Negro has been stripped of his only power to support or check that administration. Neither education nor money will settle the question without the ballot; for a ballotless group cannot command the resources of public education, and a subject and helpless class by growing richer only endangers its life by becoming a more tempting prey to any powerful oppressor. . . . A disfranchised group could fare much better under hereditary independent rulers than under elective obligated officers. The very advantages of a democracy make disfranchisement therein the worst of tyrannies.

—William Pickens,[5] 1915

REFLECTION: In an all-Black community, one young man decided to take on the white political boss who had controlled the district like a fiefdom for decades. The boss made his usual campaign stops, dispensing a few favors and patronage jobs.

Meanwhile, the young Black candidate effectively addressed the corruption of the boss's administration, but was stunned at the lack of enthusiasm from the community. One voter told him: "You're not going to get in so it would be a waste to vote for you." Another said: "I'm voting for the white man because I know what he's capable of. I don't know nothing about you except a lot of talk." The incumbent won by a landslide.

The young Black man withdrew from politics, taking the loss as a confirmation of his racial inferiority. Six months into his new term, the old boss was indicted for embezzlement of federal and municipal funds—but he handpicked his successor.

If political progress is to occur, the voiceless and the powerless must stifle the inner demons that whisper, "You don't deserve anything more than what you already have."

I'm willing to make my voice heard in my community. There is no reason for me to accept powerlessness.

POLITICAL FRIENDS

The time has come now when the Negro asks no favors because he is colored, but he is willing to stand or fall upon his merits in the great battle of life and prove by his brains, his ambition, his pluck, his perseverance, his integrity, his patriotism, that he is a man created in the image of God, with all the attributes of true manhood. . . .

In politics today the Negro is a very important factor. This is acknowledged by distinguished statesmen and politicians, for he is fast learning to think and act for himself. He has made up his mind that he will no longer bow down and be the slave of any party, that he will no longer support any man for public office who is an enemy of the race.

—*Edward Everett Brown,*[6] *1888*

REFLECTION: A new day faces us. In the current political climate, African Americans are too often regarded as perpetual wards of the state. Politically, we could attain as much legislative power as Blacks gained in Edward Everett Brown's post-Reconstruction era, but our vast numbers remain fragmented and unorganized. We shun the work needed to become involved in the electoral process.

We cannot afford to back down when so much is at stake. We cannot support the allegations that we are weak and cannot stand alone. We would be a force to be taken seriously if we massed our support behind those who hold our best interests at heart. It's foolish for us to allow our foes and "friends of the moment" to purchase our favor, our votes. We're facing grave challenges that threaten our very existence. In the past, we were locked into supporting those politicians who were our friends previously. Today, we must apply singer Janet Jackson's axiom: "What have you done for me lately?" Everyone must be scrutinized. Every offer made to us must be examined closely. We can no longer settle for leftovers. We must take our rightful place at the table.

We won't be seduced by empty slogans or hollow promises. We will support those who support us.

RACE UNITY

The time has come for us as a people to stop skylarking with ourselves and allowing others to make mimics of us. Little groups of individuals fighting against themselves can only represent themselves, they can accomplish very little in the interest of a great race scattered over the country, and for that matter, scattered over the universe. If conditions are such as to affect the race generally, then the race must organize generally to bring about a change in the conditions.

—Marcus Garvey,[7] 1921

REFLECTION: While the conditions for many African Americans worsen, we are dismayed at the petty bickering and useless games of one-upmanship practiced by some leaders in key organizations. One leader leaves a national constituency under a cloud of financial misconduct, while another is hounded as a racist for making controversial statements. Black representatives in Congress no longer speak with one voice.

For the invisible man and woman in the community, these are troubling times of mounting social and political problems. There doesn't seem to be anyone at the helm to articulate the general needs of our communities. Who will speak for us? It's up to each of us to begin organizing our communities around the issues that threaten our survival. We must start at the grassroots level and take the lead.

Where clear thought and committed action surrender to indecision and discord, there can be no unity or advancement. I will take responsibility for organizing my community.

THE RIGHT TO BEAR ARMS

A government which has power to tax a man in peace, draft him in war, should have power to defend his life in the hour of peril. A government which can protect and defend its citizens from wrong and outrage and does not is vicious. A government which would do it and cannot is weak; and where human life is insecure through either weakness or viciousness in the administration of law, there must be a lack of justice and where this is wanting, nothing can make up the deficiency.

—*Frances Ellen Watkins Harper,*[8] *1891*

REFLECTION: Handguns kill hundreds of people every week in this country. Weapons flood our streets, and no one is safe. Yet the government seems powerless to stop their fatal onslaught. Those who worship firearms are so well organized and powerful that the government cowers before their mighty influence.

Who is there to tell our children that every choice offered by a gun is a bad one? Who can console a grieving mother for the loss of her young son in a drive-by shooting? Who can reason with a husband mourning the loss of his pregnant wife to a stray bullet? Not one biblical verse advocates the so-called "God-given right" to bear arms. What will it take for our government to stand up and protect all of its citizens? We must actively campaign for stronger gun-control legislation. Our lives depend on it.

Where the greed for power and a love of weapons join, no human life is safe or secure.

SELF-DETERMINATION

*None of us can be strong unless we have the support of the commu-
nity. And unless the community is strong, it's impossible for us to be
strong. No matter how big we become.*

*We also have to stop thinking that white people are the ones to
save us. We are one of the few peoples on the face of the earth who
do not worship a God that reflects us. As long as we keep kneeling
to a white male figure, how are we going to overcome the feeling that
this white male is superior to us? The power structure is not going
to save us—never has and never will. We have to take things into
our own hands and save ourselves.*

—Camille Cosby,[9] 1989

REFLECTION: An old deacon in my childhood church, Deacon Finley, known for his curt tongue and keen insights, once told the congregation: "Never trust someone who is always linking up his future with someone he doesn't know." He was referring to the white councilman who represented our area. Deacon Finley didn't trust the man, who would appear at our church at election time, rain his weak promises upon us, then disappear until the next election day.

When a Black candidate suddenly decided to run against the white incumbent, it was the elders who organized church members and other neighbors to transport them to the polling places. The veteran politician conceded his loss with a backhanded compliment: "Maybe it's a new day, because this boy seems to speak their language while I do not."

Find someone who speaks your language. Someone who understands you and your needs. When your community has a sickness of the soul, find a healer in your midst. We can use resources found within our own community for our salvation and healing. We need not wait for others to come to our aid. We can indeed take matters into our own hands and save ourselves.

As a community we have the power to heal ourselves. We need not wait for others to provide the cure.

"YOU HAD YOUR CHANCE"

Guilt is heavy in America, and the only way to throw off this burden is by changing the conditions that created it. But first there must be acknowledgment. Since the eighties, acknowledgment has diminished. Black people are told: "We gave you your chance and you failed." The truth is, we did not fail. They never lived up to anything they wrote down. America has never repented for what it's done to our people. Or shall we talk of the Indians and broken treaties? Our society has never lived up to anything they've said to anybody of color. So it's not a matter of "We gave you." They haven't given us nothin'. You cannot rob me and give me anything. If I rob you on the corner and then say, "Here's five dollars," it's absurd.

—Reverend C. T. Vivian,[10] 1992

REFLECTION: The new battle cry among many angry whites is, "You had your chance." At a time when there is less of the American pie to be divided up, those in power have found a new way to divert attention from the fact that this democracy has not served everyone equally. The fact that so many of us, Black and white, are ill-equipped for the rigorous demands of a new millennium has less to do with race and preference than with money and affluence. Being middle class is no longer safe terrain. The middle class is dangerously close to assuming many of the characteristics of the poor.

What is the remedy? Conservatives point again at the Blacks, women, and other minorities, playing on the racial and social fears of white males. They abolish as many civil liberties as possible, turning back the clock. Conservative America insists there is a new sense of fairness which stresses merit in a color-blind society that will return us to the "good old days." We must prepare to face this challenge with a strong resolve and unbending determination.

Whether we've had our chance or not, we must adapt and change to remain a strong and competitive people.

THE NEW SMALL WORLD

It is time that we had become politicians, we mean, to understand the political economy and domestic policy of nations; that we had become as well as moral theorists, also the practical demonstrators of equal rights and self-government. Except we do, it is idle to talk about rights, it is mere chattering for the sake of being seen and heard—like the slave, saying something because his so called "master" said it, and saying just what he told him to say. Have we got now sufficient intelligence among us to understand our true position, to realise our actual condition, and determine for ourselves what is best to be done? If we have not now, we never shall have, and should at once cease prating about our equality, capacity, and all that.

—Martin R. Delany,[11] 1852

REFLECTION: "It's stupid for us to concern ourselves about all the madness going on in the world," I recently heard one Black man tell another in Harlem. "When I vote for these brothers to go to Congress, I pay them to keep an eye on things for me."

How shortsighted! When are we going to realize that it's vital for us to be full participants in the world outside our community? It's embarrassing how few of us can name five African nations, yet we claim the continent as our ancestral home. By not knowing about the larger world, we forfeit our right to have a say in how it is governed. If we are not prepared to speak up, others will speak for us.

Only a fool believes that his life isn't affected by what happens outside of it. We give up our power to decide what's best for our lives by not keeping abreast of the world's events. We must be informed about everything that goes on in the world because today what you don't know can kill you.

The world is larger than my local community. I must stay informed and involved because what happens over there affects me here.

Part 2

CREATIVITY
AND CULTURE

AFRICAN RHYTHMS

I'm convinced that we are only an extension of African civilization, and all this music is really African music. In Africa, there's music for everything—if someone is sick, it's not enough just to treat them with herbs, they must have music also. And African people are more attuned to nature—they would tune their instruments to the birds. I have tapes of forest sounds in Africa, and you can hear the rhythms of the insects and the animals like a tremendous nature symphony. Even the instruments in Africa are made from plant life, and each instrument has its own spirit—before you touch an instrument you must first praise God. These are the sorts of things you learn about the spirituality of music.

But what happens when African people come into contact with other cultures and civilizations? They merely take them over and make them their own. I'm sure that many of us come from families of musicians that go back hundreds of years, and that the spirit forces of our ancestors come out in us centuries later. . . . We all have music in us—your heartbeat is your drum, your voice is your sound—and music is supposed to put you in tune with nature.

—Randy Weston,[1] 1979

REFLECTION: African rhythms are apparent in our talk, our walk, our mannerisms, and our sense of style. There's even a musical pulse in our relationships. Somehow the larger society has been unable to condition this trait out of us. The phenomenon of our polyrhythmic existence has been studied and analyzed in great detail, but somehow its essence has always eluded our observers.

Famed big band leader Count Basie always told his men while they were revving up to perform: "Play like you think!" We are indeed an African people. It's in our bodies, our minds, our hearts, our souls. It's how we view our world. This does not mean that every Black man and woman can get funky or that all of us understand the lexicon of the drum. It means that we have a deep, intuitive appreciation for the music of life. The spirit of the drum is with us every time we open our mouths to speak or sing. It's there every time we move our bodies to dance. We are African rhythms made flesh!

We honor the spirit of our ancestors in the rhythms of our lives.

CULTURE

Our music, our dance, is worth more than all the cotton ever picked, all the tobacco ever planted. We have given America more than it could ever have stolen from us, free. What would they be doing, what would they be dancing, what would they be singing, what would music be? They'd still be square dancing! We have given that. We should celebrate ourselves. We should understand what we've done and what we have. We are the most communicative people in the world, the most entertaining people in the world. . . .

. . . Culture is the sum of your experiences. What you've been through and how you express that in painting, poetry, playwriting or however. That is your culture. I think that this is the other thing that unifies Black people; it is our common culture. In addition to our common oppression, we have a common culture.

—Oscar Brown, Jr.,[2] 1976

REFLECTION: For a long time, we were brainwashed to believe that our culture had no value. When gathered together, we sang its praises, but when others told us that it did not compare to European culture, we remained silent. The impact of African American culture has been unequaled in its far-reaching influence and tremendous global appeal. People pay to hear our music, read our words, watch us dance, or see our films.

Perhaps it's our history of oppression that has given us this uncommon talent to create art that is strikingly original and deceptively complex. Our cultural imagination constantly renews America's artistic vision. No matter what the form of cultural expression, once we touch it, it is never the same. We are that powerful!

I am proud of the tremendous contributions of African American culture. It speaks to the world of who we are in a way that nothing else does.

BLACK HISTORY

In Europe and Japan they respect black people's culture, what we have contributed to the world. They know what it is. But white Americans would rather push a white person like Elvis Presley, who is just a copy of a black person, than to push the real thing. They give all this money to white rock groups, to promote and publicize them, give them a lot of awards for trying to be like black artists. But that's all right because everyone knows that Chuck Berry started the shit, not Elvis. They know Duke Ellington was "the King of Jazz" and not Paul Whiteman. Everybody knows that. But you won't see it in the history books unless we get the power to write our own history and tell our story ourselves. Nobody else is going to do it for us and do it like it is supposed to be done.

—Miles Davis,[3] 1989

REFLECTION: In 1927, prominent historian Carter G. Woodson explained the importance of our history somewhat differently than jazz trumpeter Miles Davis. He said, "We should not emphasize Negro History but the Negro in history." The role of the African American has been significant in the history of this country and the history of the world. But, for the most part, we have not been able to glorify and dignify our own story. While countless books have been written about us, most have been factually incorrect or burdened with a malicious social agenda. Many history books merely record African American achievements as a footnote to the excellence of others.

Very few accounts show us as pioneers, inventors, or leaders. But we've allowed this to happen. We must tell our own stories, define our own place in the pages of history, and set the tempo of our march toward destiny. We must document the joy of our victories, record the measure of our strength and valor in times of challenge. We must pick our own heroes and heroines. No one must be allowed to do these crucial things for us. No one knows us the way we know ourselves.

I will write my own history, set my own standards, define my own worth.

CREATIVITY

Creativity is something that can happen only in the mind. It doesn't matter whether you're dealing with clay or paints or words or just your way of living. . . . we are the most creative people in the world, which is an extraordinary thing. We can take pig intestines and make them into such an incredible dish that you forget where they came from and what you're eating.

—Bill Gunn,[4] 1973

REFLECTION: Not long ago, a Creole chef praised the creativity that goes into the cooking of soul food, amazed at how so much could be done with so little. Black people have always been able to improvise, to create, to expand richly on an original theme and take it where it has never gone before. It is our creativity that lets us know that the Creator is present in our lives. In so many areas, we have been able to share that creativity and originality with the world.

All of us are creative; however, most of us do not see this in ourselves or choose not to develop it. When we cultivate that creativity, we break free of old beliefs and barriers. When we're creative, we build something glorious and new by blending the past and present into an expression of the future. We affirm God in our lives each time we create something that never existed before.

By being creative today, I celebrate the Creator's presence in my life with a gift for the world.

THE WISDOM OF THE BLUES

Our blues at the time was our need to ignore the reality of our situation. The situation was as unreal as our existing reality. Blues which Ralph Ellison has described as suppressed intellectual energy expressed physically. What we had learned in the early fifties was to express all those problems we had at that early age, all those problems we knew existed with our mothers and fathers, our sisters and cousins, our aunts and uncles; what we had learned was to hide it from that other world in another life style. The ability to hide it was our rhythm. The knowledge of it was our blues.

—Woodie King, Jr.,[5] 1974

REFLECTION: The blues is at the core of the African American spirit, with its yearning for fulfillment, its ability to survive against all the odds. Faced with overwhelming adversity, Black bluesmen and women blended the solemn, regal cry of the African griots—who sang of the unending search for truth, affirmation, and goodness amid a life of tragedy, turmoil, and sudden change—with the liberating rhythms of nature. They transformed what others condemned as the Devil's music to unparalleled artistic heights. The blues has always helped us to make sense out of the senseless and to keep on keepin' on.

Black people have always added a sense of transcendence to that haunting feeling of "downheartedness." The blues embodies the resilient, creative, and unconquerable spirit that has allowed us to survive our forced passage from Africa to the plantation, the tragedy of Civil War, Reconstruction, and the battles of the Civil Rights Movement. They will continue to sustain us as we face our current socioeconomic crisis.

I will learn to listen to the wisdom of the blues.

POSITIVE SELF-IMAGE

For if we can, in fact, create for our own people, work for our own people, belong to our own people, we will no longer be forced into artistic prostitution and self-betrayal in the mad scramble, imposed upon us far too long, to belong to some other people. We can indeed, as long as we truly deserve the support of our own, embrace our blackness and find the stuff of our manhood.

The Negro people, if given a chance, will cherish, defend, and protect its own. . . . If we turn to them ever so little, they will turn to us in full. It is time for us, who call ourselves artists, scholars, and thinkers, to rejoin the people from whom we came. We shall then and only then be free to tell the truth about our people, and that truth shall make us free!

Only then can we begin to take a truly independent position within the confines of American culture, a black position. And from that position, walk, talk, think, fight, and create like men. Respectful of all, sharing with any, but beholden to none save our own.

—Ossie Davis,[6] 1964

REFLECTION: Most Black people understand the works of African American artists on a soul level. When we create Black art and culture, their values are not a mystery to us. We understand the passionate spirit fueling the artistic expression. The work of Aretha Franklin, Charlie Parker, or B. B. King never needs any explanation—because the raw power of their music speaks to the truth of our shared experience. To other ears, such soul music may sound like sheer noise, but to many of us, it is a gift that expands, enriches, and energizes our collective spirit.

When Black culture is sold to a larger audience, it often gets artificially flavored and loses its vitality. We must strive to create our art and define its value from a truly independent position—beholden to no one—so that our artistic treasures can be purely preserved for generations to come.

Today I will celebrate the artistic gifts of my race by fully expressing my blackness.

BLACK ART

So it must be with the Negro artist—he must not be content with merely recording a scene as a machine. He must enter wholeheartedly into the situation which he wishes to convey. The artist must be the medium through which humanity expresses itself. In this sense the greatest artists have faced the realities of life, and have been profoundly social.

I don't mean by this that the Negro artist should confine himself only to such scenes as lynchings, or policemen clubbing workers. . . . If it is the race question, the social struggle, or whatever else that needs expression, it is to that the artist must surrender himself. An intense, eager devotion to present day life, to study it, to help relieve it, this is the calling of the Negro artist.

—Romare Bearden,[7] 1934

REFLECTION: Some cultural critics would have us believe that all Black art and culture is equal. Not true. Much of it does no honor to its creators or its audience. These "art for art's sake" theorists fail to recognize that the soul of art and the flame of imagination come from a higher realm.

Meaningful art, guided by superior imagination, celebrates the basic truths of daily life. These creations offer us new concepts and ideas to consider, new worlds to explore, and they profoundly affect our total being.

Unfortunately, a growing number of African American artists are only concerned with "making it." Where older revered artists celebrated the joy and transcendence of the ordinary, some contemporary artists seek favor and commercial gain by depicting the sensational. What such inauthentic artists produce is an incomplete and distorted picture of the "realities of life" in the Black community. Their work is an embarrassment to all of the great Black artists who preceded them. Art and imagination, when fully realized, release tremendous restorative powers.

Great art can nourish and fortify my soul. I take pride and pleasure in the finest expressions of Black artists.

CULTURAL CRITICISM

The danger of writing about the past, as I have done, is romanticizing it. I don't think I do that, but I do feel that people were more interesting then than they are now. It seems to me there were more excesses in women and men, and people accepted them as they don't know. In the black community where I grew up, there were eccentricity and freedom, less conformity in individual habits—but close conformity in terms of survival of the village, of the tribe. Before sociological microscopes were placed on us, people did anything and nobody was run out of town.

—Toni Morrison,[8] *1993*

REFLECTION: Nobel Laureate author Toni Morrison is correct when she says we once accepted the full spectrum of behavior within our community. While Morrison calls for acceptance and tolerance of excess and eccentricity, she does not rule out the need for constructive criticism within our African American community. Criticism can be a valuable tool in personal growth, but it should be used wisely. Criticism should not be mean-spirited or rooted in finding fault or in one-upmanship. It's about providing guidance to help each other take another look at our words or deeds.

None of us likes to be criticized, so we need to offer criticism with care and diplomacy. Our intention should never be to merely point out what's wrong but rather to assist the person in assessing their choices and to help measure how closely they came to actually meeting their goal.

Often in the Black community, we see things going awry and say nothing. At other times, we criticize loudly and purposelessly when we should keep quiet. We need to remember to use criticism as a powerful catalyst for our individual and collective growth.

I offer criticism constructively and with sensitivity.

THE SOURCE

I worked from my own community; from within my own community. That was the motivating factor, the source.

Although my content is very regional, I would hope that regardless of what period, what age, or what people come in contact with it, there would be an understanding and an appreciation for this work even though its original source was regional. In order to achieve this, I would have to grow. Growth is a continual thing; it doesn't stop. We can only reflect our own experience, but we would hope that that would be understood by others, universally, beyond the source. To me, this is important.

—Jacob Lawrence,[9] 1977

REFLECTION: When one sees the strength and pride in Jacob Lawrence's paintings, one understands his relationship with the Source. Our power comes from our people, our community. In all we do, the power of that Source is there. It is that part of us that no one can degrade or destroy. It is that part of us that could not be enslaved. It is that part of us that our enemies fear most. It is that sense of Oneness that contradicts the feeling of Otherness we often experience in the outside world. The Source is our heart, our soul.

With the power of our Source behind us, in us, we cannot help but succeed; we have seen what happens to those of us who sever our ties to it. For this reason, our people must remain close spiritually. We must treat the power of the Source with respect and reverence. We must treasure it in our daily lives.

I revere the power of the Source, which is the strength of my people.

CULTURE AS SOUL FOOD

There is the culture starved black community with its complexities and its tremendous need for visual art, more so because of the mesmerizing effect of commercial television. The black artist is seeking more and more to move within this community. He is investigating our past and interpreting history to awaken us to our great cultural heritage, giving us an additional weapon with which to combat racist historical myths. There is no question as to who we are and where we are going—black people on our way to liberation.

We must learn from inside the struggle because of its changes as the people change. Only as a part of the mass can we recognize its needs as to our artistic contribution. Because art needs to be public to reach the majority of blacks, regardless of class, the artists are taking art to the streets in mural painting, to the churches and other meeting places. . . . We must go where black people are.

—Elizabeth Catlett,[10] *1975*

REFLECTION: Arthur Mitchell, founder and director of the Dance Theater of Harlem, often talks about the need to make the arts and culture accessible to the people in the community. "Take away the culture and you deprive a people of everything that nourishes them," he says. "It's important that they see their lives, their struggles, their triumphs reflected back to them through their culture."

For this reason, Mitchell opens the doors of his center to the people of the Harlem community several times a year so that his neighbors can witness the glorious creativity of their culture. In turn, the people of the community, many of them of meager means, have been supportive of the dance troupe in every way possible.

Culture defines how we live and how we grow. If you're an artist, take your plays, your films, your poems, your music, your dance into the community. There is an eager audience there just waiting to welcome you home.

Black culture is the soul food of my people.

A DIVERSE PEOPLE

The Negro Race in this land must repudiate this absurd notion which is stealing on the American mind. The Race must declare that it is not to be put into a single groove; and for the simple reason (1) that man was made by his Maker to traverse the whole circle of existence, above as well as below; and that universality is the kernel of all true civilization, of all race elevation. And (2) that the Negro mind, imprisoned for nigh three hundred years, needs breadth and freedom, largeness, altitude, and elasticity; not stint nor rigidity, nor contractedness.

—Alexander Crummell,[11] 1898

REFLECTION: African Americans come in a wide variety of shades and temperaments. They come from many places around the world, and reflect many cultural and racial mixtures. Some of us love blues, fried okra, and saucy barbecue ribs. Others love jazz, salsa, and reggae. And there are those who might prefer Bach and B. B. King, or caviar and chitlins. We are a collection of people as diverse as any other. So when you hear someone saying that he totally understands "the African American mind," scrutinize anything he says.

There is no single type of African American. I treasure the rich diversity of my people.

A WORLD OF VALUE

I must see my understandings produce results in human experience. Productivity is my first value. I must make and mould and build life. As an artist, I must shape human relationships. To me, life itself is the greatest material. I would far rather form a man than form a book. My whole being is devoted to making my small area of existence a work of art.

I am building a world.

—Jean Toomer,[12] 1929

REFLECTION: Novelist Jean Toomer, noted for his classic work *Cane*, wrote about the need to elevate the purpose of our lives above the usual pursuit of the dollar. Blind materialism rarely offers us the kind of positive outlets that allow us to tap into the totality of who we are. How many of us work for forty years without stopping to cultivate human relationships outside of the family or workplace?

It's not enough to fill our homes with pretty and costly things. We must be conscious of how we live, of the colors we use on the canvas of our lives. We must open ourselves up to new experiences, new adventures, new friendships. We must free ourselves from the prison of ego and habit and re-shape our ideas of who we are.

The artful life begins when we take dreams hidden within us and bring them to life. Life as art affirms the best that is in us.

My life is a work of art.

Part 3

SELF-ESTEEM

SELF-KNOWLEDGE

There is much misunderstanding among us because of our inferior knowledge of self. We have been to schools where they do not teach us the knowledge of self. We have been to schools of our slave-master children. We have been to their schools and gone as far as they allowed us to go. That was not far enough for us to learn a knowledge of self. The lack of knowledge of self is one of our main handicaps. It blocks us throughout the world. If you were the world and you were a part of the world, you would also turn a man down if he did not know who he actually was. If we, the so-called Negroes, do not know our own selves, how can we be accepted by a people who have a knowledge of self?

—The Honorable Elijah Muhammad,[1] *1965*

REFLECTION: Robbed of our history, robbed of our languages, robbed of our culture, we have lost our true knowledge of self. The history of Black people in America is but a brief chapter in our history as a race. We are the earth's original people, the wellspring of humanity. And yet we have been tragically dispossessed of our true selves in this country.

It is only by reclaiming the truth of our history that we can develop a deep, honest understanding of ourselves, first as a race, then as individuals. This is the key to racial self-esteem. That we have achieved as much as we have under such adverse circumstances is powerful evidence of who we can become once we have reclaimed our rightful heritage.

As Elijah Muhammad said: "It is time for us to learn who we really are, and it is time for us to understand ourselves." This knowledge of self will allow us to see our lives in their proper perspective, not only internally but in the external world as well.

Today, I will reclaim the knowledge of our lost Black heritage and walk with pride in the world.

THE POWER OF SPIRIT

The power of spirit that our people have is intangible, but it is a great force that must be unleashed in the struggles of today. A spirit of steadfast determination, exaltation in the face of trials—it is the very soul of our people that has been formed through all the long and weary years of our march toward freedom. It is the deathless spirit of the great ones who have led our people in the past— Douglass, Tubman and all the others—and of the millions who kept "a-inching along." That spirit lives in our people's songs—in the sublime grandeur of "Deep River," in the driving power of "Jacob's Ladder," in the militancy of "Joshua Fit the Battle of Jericho," and in the poignant beauty of all our spirituals. . . .

Yes, that power of the spirit is the pride and glory of my people, and there is no human quality in all of America that can surpass it. It is a force only for good: there is no hatefulness about it. It exalts the finest things of life—justice and equality, human dignity and fulfillment. It is of the earth, deeply rooted, and it reaches up to the highest skies and mankind's noblest aspirations. It is time for this spirit to be evoked and exemplified in all we do, for it is a force mightier than all our enemies and will triumph over all their evil ways.

—Paul Robeson,[2] 1958

REFLECTION: We forget we are descendants of a mighty and proud race, a people who have created strong civilizations and rich cultures. We forget these facts of our lineage when we think small and fail to take responsibility for our actions every day. We forget all of this when we dwell on our separateness and partial acceptance in the white world.

Our spirit, forged by the contradiction of our existence in this nation, is so strong and powerful that nothing can turn us around if we heed its call. It is the dynamic force which will carry us forward in the severest times of stress and oppression, much as it did Douglass, Tubman, Truth, and others. No political or military might can subdue it. It is this power which anchors our belief in the promise of our future. It is this power which lets us know that justice and human dignity always prevail. If we evoke this spirit in our daily lives, we can turn aside any foe, any obstacle.

Nothing can conquer my powerful spirit.

SELF-ESTEEM

I looked up into her face and repeated: "Tell me, mother, am I a nigger?" There were tears in her eyes and I could see that she was suffering for me. And then it was that I looked at her critically for the first time. I had thought of her in a childish way only as the most beautiful woman in the world; now I looked at her searching for defects. I could see that her skin was almost brown, that her hair was not so soft as mine, and that she did differ in some way from the other ladies who came to the house; yet, even so, I could see that she was very beautiful, more beautiful than any of them. She must have felt that I was examining her, for she hid her face in my hair and said with difficulty: "No, my darling, you are not a nigger." She went on: "You are as good as anybody; if anyone calls you a nigger, don't notice them."

—James Weldon Johnson,[3] 1912

REFLECTION: A few Christmases ago, a white Santa Claus made the national news when a video camera captured him hoisting a small Black child onto his lap and calling him a little monkey. He never thought about the power of those words to maim the soul and spirit of the youngster. When Marge Schott uses the word "nigger" to describe the Black players on her Cincinnati Reds baseball team, it damages young African American fans all over the country. Richard Pryor, during the latter part of his career, stopped using the word to characterize his people.

The effects of abusive language are very painful and life-destroying. Demeaning words and disparaging labels create a cancer that kills us all. We must all be mindful of the words we use to label ourselves and our people. The self-esteem of our race is at stake.

I will choose my words carefully because they carry the power to hurt or heal my people.

SECOND SIGHT

If you're born black in America you must quickly teach yourself to recognize the invisible barriers disciplining the space in which you may move. This seventh sense you must activate is imperative for survival and sanity. Nothing is what it seems. You must always take second readings, decode appearances, pick out the obstructions erected to keep you in your place. Then work around them. What begins as a pragmatic reaction to race prejudice gradually acquires the force of an instinctive response. A special way of seeing becomes second nature. You ignore the visible landscape. It has nothing to do with you; it will never change, so you learn a kind of systematic skepticism, a stoicism, and if you're lucky, ironic detachment. I can't get to the mountain and the mountain ain't hardly coming to me no matter how long I sit here and holler, so mize well do what I got to do right here on level ground and leave the mountain to them folks think they own it.

—John Edgar Wideman,[4] 1985

REFLECTION: I remember going to the store with my mother as a boy. I watched her select items and wheel them up front to the checkout counter. Just as she was ready to place a package of strawberries on the conveyor belt, she noticed the berries were rotten and moldy underneath the top ones, which looked firm and ripe. She told this to the white cashier.

The woman said, "They're good enough for you to eat. Besides, I'll give you a discount." Without a word, my mother took the berries from her and set them aside.

In the car, my mother turned to me and said: "She wouldn't have done that to a white woman." What I learned in that moment was that I was not inferior to anyone else, that I didn't have to accept disrespect from anyone.

Many Blacks still haven't internalized that lesson. We must never accept a mind-set which whispers to us that we're second-rate, that we're not good enough. We must never allow ourselves to be given less because we think we're worth less. We are the best. We deserve the best. No one is superior to us—and we should act accordingly.

I will not be treated with disrespect. I am not inferior to anyone.

HUE AND CRY

Now I was also learning that the world had decided that we were all Negro, but that some of us were more Negro than others. The whole system at that time was saying to us that you achieved more, you went further, you had a better chance, you got the awards, if you were not black-black with kinky hair. Black was bad and you didn't want to be black, and so the message we were getting was that you were really in tough shape and it was too bad that you were so unfortunate that your skin was totally black and there was no light there anywhere.

—Barbara Jordan,[5] 1979

REFLECTION: Some of the cruelest acts performed against African Americans have been executed by members of our own tribe. We learned too well at the master's knee to determine worth by the color of our skin. "If you're Black, get back!" Those who resembled the master in skin color and facial features were given the honored place among the powerless.

Today, decades after "Black is beautiful," skin color madness has returned. Many Blacks refuse to hire a dark-skinned sister to work at the front desk. Some families frown if their high-toned princess brings home a young man two shades blacker than she. Parents have been known to favor the children with the "fairer skin" over their darker offspring.

Sometimes the echo of the lash can be heard in our souls long after the cruel instrument has been put away. We must stop punishing ourselves for having survived.

Letting go of self-destructive behavior frees me to look at myself with new eyes and to live in the world in new ways.

"DO US PROUD"

Tell them that the sacrifice was not in vain. Tell them that by habits of thrift and economy, by the way of the industrial school and college, we are coming. We are crawling up, working up, bursting up: coming through oppression, unjust discrimination and prejudice, but through them all we are coming up, and with proper habits, intelligence and property, there is no power on earth that can permanently stay our progress.

—Booker T. Washington,[6] 1896

REFLECTION: Years ago, Andrew Young, then U.S. Ambassador to the United Nations, was walking down a hall in the mammoth assembly building, heading to a press conference. A pack of reporters and cameramen dogged his footsteps, yelling questions and comments at his back. Young kept walking.

As the corridor turned toward the main lobby, the Ambassador spotted an old Black man carrying two brooms near the banks of elevators. Young stopped to shake the man's hand. With pride gleaming on his face, the elderly Black man winked at the striding Young and calmly said: "You go get them, boy. Do us proud."

A smile split Young's face and he nodded to one of his aides, saying, "See, it's people like him that make me able to put up with this foolishness."

There is no present achievement of our race that was not built on the sweat and sacrifice of those who have gone before us.

Whenever I tire, I will contemplate the countless sacrifices of my elders.

HUMANITY OF THE POOR

To be poor, is to be hungry without possible hope of food; to be sick without hope of medicine; to be tired and sleepy without a place to lay one's head; to be naked without the hope of clothing; to be despised and comfortless. To be poor is to be a fit subject for crime and hell.

The hungry man steals bread and thereby breaks the eighth commandment; by his state he breaks all the laws of God and man and becomes an outcast. In thought and deed he covets his neighbor's goods; comfortless as he is he seeks his neighbor's wife; to him there is no other course but sin and death. That is the way of poverty. No one wants to be poor.

—Marcus Garvey,[7] 1923

REFLECTION: The number of poor people grows each year. More and more formerly productive persons find themselves suddenly without an economic safety net or a home as factories close and companies reduce their labor force. Many of these people have never filed for unemployment compensation or applied for food stamps.

These newly minted poor people once believed the media's images of the impoverished as welfare queens with five babies. Now they dread the day that they'll be forced to live in a shelter or sleep in their car. Once their savings disappear and everything of value has been sold to pay their mortgage, they will learn that the poor have very few friends. A person's worth has nothing to do with his income. As the redistribution of wealth occurs around the world, many of us will discover that we are two paychecks away from poverty.

No one chooses a leaky roof or an empty stomach. God, help me to have a compassionate heart for those who live in lack and deep suffering.

SELF-LOVE

Sometimes you'd think I have more children than anyone in Mississippi, but I love them and want to help them, for they are the leaders of tomorrow. I see some little kids just six years old and they already look defeated. I just want them to feel proud to be human beings, whether they're black as this skillet or white as that stove. So you see, it's important for me to stay here, because I'm not actually living for myself. If I left, there would be so many children who'd have no way of knowing life doesn't have to be a tragedy because they're black.

—Fannie Lou Hamer,[8] 1966

REFLECTION: Self-loathing is never pretty. Psychologist Kenneth Clark saw it years ago in experiments where young Black girls were offered a choice of black or white dolls to play with. The girls always selected the white dolls first. They wouldn't even touch the dark-skinned dolls. Today, our self-hatred is taking even more tragic forms: drug addiction, violence, and broken families.

Being Black is not a tragedy—but being lost with no sense of self or community is. . . . Our youth have heard us say, "I'm Black and I'm proud" for generations. But now we have to live it. We cannot allow self-hatred and defeatism to beat down on the heads and hearts of our children like an endless rain. Every effort must be made to teach them how to love themselves before the loathing rots the foundation of their souls.

Today, I will ease the pain of self-hatred by showing a young person the power of self-respect and self-love.

DIGNITY

A colored comedy act was going on as I sat down. They were funny and I was laughing, but I wasn't enjoying myself. Something was bothering me. I listened to them saying, "Ladies and gen'men, we's gwine git our laigs movin' heah." They were talking "colored" as Negro acts always did. I'd heard it a thousand times before, but for the first time it jarred me. I watched them doing all the colored clichés, realizing that we were doing exactly the same thing. We'd always done them. It was the way people expected Negro acts to be, so that's the way we were. But why can't we say "gentlemen"? Why must it be "gen'men"? Must we downgrade ourselves? Must we be caricatures of cotton-field slaves? Can't we entertain and still keep our dignity? We were contributing a means for mockery by characterizing all Negroes as shuffling illiterates who carried razors, shot craps, lied, and ate nothing but watermelon and fried chicken.

—Sammy Davis, Jr.,[9] 1989

REFLECTION: In the early years of this century Bert Williams, an articulate and gifted performer, earned top dollar as a minstrel, clowning as a Black man imitating a white man imitating a Black man.

Even though his act was an unqualified success, he soon tired of the routine and began to add a deeper humanity to his performance. That alienated his many white fans, who wondered why Williams would tamper with a sure thing. Williams replied: "I grew tired of playing the fool." Like Sammy Davis, Jr., he asked himself, Why can't I just entertain and still keep my dignity?

I refuse to accept or perpetuate false, negative images of myself or my people no matter how lucrative the rewards.

CLASS CONSCIOUSNESS

"My people! My people!" From the earliest rocking of my cradle days, I have heard this cry go up from Negro lips. It is forced outward by pity, scorn and hopeless resignation. It is called forth by the observations of one class of Negro on the doings of another branch of the brother in black. For instance, well-mannered Negroes groan out like that when they board a train or a bus and find other Negroes on there with their shoes off, stuffing themselves with fried fish, bananas and peanuts, and throwing the garbage on the floor. Maybe they are not only eating and drinking. The offenders may be "loud-talking" the place, and holding back nothing of their private lives, in a voice that embraces the entire coach. The well-dressed Negro shrinks back in his seat at that, shakes his head and sighs, "My people! My people!"

—Zora Neale Hurston,[10] 1942

REFLECTION: They dress differently than us. They speak differently than us. They walk differently than us. We cringe when we hear someone else describe them: "They live in the projects—you know the type." We look at them with that judgment in mind and we're afraid that we'll be judged the same way, despite all our education, good jobs, and middle-class aspirations.

What we forget is that discrimination across class lines is as hurtful as discrimination on the basis of color. If we judge each other harshly for behavior, dress, and speech, we're buying into the false belief that poverty equals inferiority.

When we deny the humanity of others, we limit our experience of life. I will not turn my back on any of my brothers and sisters.

VICTIM NO MORE

For even as his life toughens the Negro, even as it brutalizes him, sensitizes him, dulls him, goads him to anger, moves him to irony, sometimes fracturing and sometimes affirming his hopes; even as it shapes his attitudes toward family, sex, love, religion; even as it modulates his humor, tempers his joy—it conditions him to deal with his life and with himself. Because it is his life and no mere abstraction in someone's head. He must live it and try consciously to grasp its complexity until he can change it; must live it as he changes it. He is no mere product of his socio-political predicament. He is a product of the interaction between his racial predicament, his individual will and the broader American cultural freedom in which he finds his ambiguous existence.

—*Ralph Ellison,*[11] *1963*

REFLECTION: Every life has obstacles, distractions, and challenges. The sum of our life should be measured by how we surmount and overcome the boulders in our path. But too often, our commitment to progress is undercut by our negativity, by thinking of ourselves as victims with everything against us—even God. Getting caught up in this victim trap means handing over our power to others. Sympathy for a victim erodes quickly. No one ever sees a victim on equal footing with themselves—victims can make few demands that anyone will honor.

A brother once told me: "Everything happens to Black folks. God must not like us too tough. You don't see what we face happening to whites." Not true. Whites have their own share of disasters and tragedies to bear. Our energy and focus must not be wasted on counting who sheds the most tears or who suffers the greatest pain. We are survivors, not victims! There is no quit in us. We must act as strivers and achievers—nothing less.

We are never without options despite the challenges that life brings.

BLACK AND BLESSED

We were always stared at. Whenever we went outside the neighborhood that knew us, we were inspected like specimens under glass. My mother prepared us. As she marched us down our front stairs, she would say what our smiles were on tiptoe to hear, "Come on children, let's go out and drive the white folks crazy."

She said it without rancor, and she said it in that outrageous way to make us laugh. She was easing our entry into a world that outranked us and outnumbered us. If she could not help us see ourselves with the humor, however wry, that gives the heart its grace, she would never have forgiven herself for letting our spirits be crushed before we had learned to sheathe them with pride.

—Dorothy West,[12] 1995

REFLECTION: Nothing is more important in life than belief in the value of yourself and your culture. In the days of our elders, there was some talk about self-pride, self-determination, and self-worth, but not with the frequency we hear today. Think about it. They didn't need to say it because they believed in themselves and in our bloodline. They believed that we're all on life's journey—whatever our hue. On this common journey, some of us would hit the mark, and some of us wouldn't. Those successes and failures were a question of character and hard work, not of color. They did not believe that anyone, or any race, was better than Black folks. They did not talk blackness—they lived it every day of their lives with a sense of dignity and pride.

Our elders didn't harp on the idea of race, because that was something that could not be changed. And who would if they could? Being Black wasn't the curse some folks thought it to be. Our elders had fun being Black. They were proud of themselves and their own and they didn't care who knew it.

I am proud of who I am and of who we are. Today I will celebrate the uniqueness of my culture.

Part 4

VALUES

THE DIGNITY OF WORK

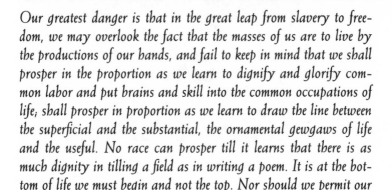

Our greatest danger is that in the great leap from slavery to free-dom, we may overlook the fact that the masses of us are to live by the productions of our hands, and fail to keep in mind that we shall prosper in the proportion as we learn to dignify and glorify com-mon labor and put brains and skill into the common occupations of life; shall prosper in proportion as we learn to draw the line between the superficial and the substantial, the ornamental gewgaws of life and the useful. No race can prosper till it learns that there is as much dignity in tilling a field as in writing a poem. It is at the bot-tom of life we must begin and not the top. Nor should we permit our grievances to overshadow our opportunities.

—Booker T. Washington,[1] *1895*

REFLECTION: Ever watch a person smile while producing something with their hands? It is the joy of doing a task and performing it well that gives us satisfaction. No job or chore is too big or too small for us not to take pride in the final accomplishment.

All work has dignity. There is nothing wrong with soiling our hands or bending our backs if it allows us to walk upright with pride and self-respect. Whenever you hear someone say Blacks are lazy or don't carry their weight, remind them of our long history of hard labor that helped to build this country. Many of us have never lost our pride in doing a good job.

I honor the value and dignity of work. Nothing can replace the pride and self-respect it brings.

THE BEST SUCCESS

It's God, man. God did it. I mean I did everything I could not to be here. Truth. I mean, I tried not to be here. It just didn't work. It must be a greater purpose. . . .

I mean, I take this seriously. No matter how frightening it gets. And it does get frightening. It is very frightening for a fifty-four-year-old person to deal with success when you've never dealt with anything but failure before. I worked *hard at failure. I mean, I worked hard at it. I gave it my best. So I'm trying to learn how to give success my best now.*

—Frank Morgan,[2] 1990

REFLECTION: Jazz saxophonist Frank Morgan's incredible life was recounted in a successful 1987 off-Broadway play, *Prison-Made Tuxedos*. He was a rising star in the music world when drug addiction and inner anguish brought him down. Morgan became addicted to heroin at age seventeen, while trying to emulate his idol, sax great Charlie Parker. His fame continued to grow in the early 1950s until a series of drug-related arrests derailed his career, landing him in prison for twenty-five years.

With determination and a new spiritual perspective, Morgan reemerged in 1985, started recording again, and conquered failure. He credits the Creator with his startling recovery and artistic rebirth. Surrendering to the worst parts of ourselves can never be an option. Morgan learned to abandon failure and to give his best to success.

I refuse to work hard at failure; I choose to give success my best.

INTEGRITY

I could make millions if I led my people the wrong way, to something I know is wrong. So now I have to make a decision. Step into a billion dollars and denounce my people or step into poverty and teach them the truth. Damn the money. Damn the heavyweight championship. I will die before I sell out my people for the white man's money. The wealth of America and the friendship of all the people who support the war would be nothing if I'm not content internally and if I'm not in accord with the will of Almighty Allah.
—Muhammad Ali,[3] 1968

REFLECTION: African Americans will always remember boxer Muhammad Ali for his legendary performances inside the ring. But it was outside the ring that Ali truly commanded our attention when he defied the U.S. government and took a stand against the war in Vietnam. Even when he was offered a fortune, he steadfastly refused to compromise his religious beliefs.

Integrity is one of the highest virtues of humankind. When we have a solid sense of self, when we know where we stand in the world, it's impossible to sway us with temptation. Integrity is the foundation of character. If we relinquish it, we lose an important part of ourselves. We are permanently weakened. When we hold fast to our values and standards, we are no longer vulnerable to the lures of others and their compromising views. Integrity gives us control over our lives. Integrity is power.

I will never sell out my beliefs and principles. I know that character and integrity are the cornerstones of an honorable life.

DECISIONS

To decide to do nothing is to make a decision, I felt. Since we have only one life and there is only one certainty in life, death, then a person must choose what he is going to do with his life. He makes that decision whether he recognizes it or not. We choose by our inaction. Therefore, we as black people had to decide what we were going to do with our black lives. This meant that each black person had to decide what he was going to do and the choice should be made in favor of service to people. We cannot fight racism and exploitation once we are dead. Action is necessary and we must carry it out now, for death always faces us. . . . When people overcome the fear of death, then and only then are they willing to lay down their lives for humanity. We as black people must develop the love for humanity which will make us act in the name of justice and die for the future of blacks and all humanity, for we are an indivisible part of mankind.

—James Forman,[4] 1972

REFLECTION: Henry Armstrong, who was the first boxer to hold three world titles at the same time, once told a reporter: "My every move is a decision. I never hesitate." In life, we are presented with an unending stream of events requiring choices and decisions, often with very little time to weigh the options. In the face of this onslaught, we sometimes become frozen in doubt and indecision. We think too much. We second-guess ourselves. Our lack of self-confidence often makes us turn to people who give us a lot of advice but very little wisdom.

Time is an important factor in the decision-making process. Too often while we're debating the problem internally, life continues on its own course and makes the decision for us. Some of us love the drama of it all, but in the end it does us no good.

Weigh your options carefully, but put a time limit on making your decision. Don't allow anyone else to make your decisions for you. Life requires nothing less.

Whatever we decide to do, we're making a decision.

SUBSTANCE

Know the difference between substance and style. Too many of us think success is a Saks Fifth Avenue charge card or a "bad" set of wheels. Now, these are things to enjoy, but they are not life goals. I was watching former President Johnson's inaugural ball on television with a Black college president's wife in Mississippi, when Mrs. [Fannie Lou] Hamer, that great lady of the Mississippi Civil Rights Movement, who lacked a college degree but certainly not intelligence or clear purpose, came onto the screen. The college president's wife moaned, "Oh my, there's Miz Hamer at the President's ball, and she doesn't even have on a long dress." My response was: "That's all right. Mrs. Hamer with no long gown is there, and you and I with our long gowns are not." So often we miss the real point—we buy BMW's and fur coats before we think about whether where we're going to drive and wear them is worthwhile. Nobody ever asks about what kind of car Ralph Bunche drove or what kind of designer suit Martin Luther King, Jr., bought. Don't confuse style with meaning. Get your insides in order and your direction clear first, and then worry about your clothes and your wheels.

—Marian Wright Edelman,[5] 1988

REFLECTION: As a young man, still in my late teens, I emigrated to Los Angeles where I lived next door to Mr. Davis, a man in his nineties. A native of New Orleans, he had lived several lifetimes in one long life. Once he had been a musician playing with Satchmo and Kid Ory. In another life, he worked as a seaman, traveling to faraway ports around the globe. In another period he served as a missionary in Manila, teaching reading and writing to the poor. Mr. Davis had many incarnations, and along the way he'd even had a wife and five children.

Often as we sat together over a meal and pored through one of Mr. Davis's countless scrapbooks, he talked about the vastness of his life and experiences.

"Be a person of depth and quality," Mr. Davis would say. "Let your interior be better than your exterior. Forget façade and front. When you see a lot of style, most of the time there's very little behind it. Seek out everything in life that will force you to be the best you can be." Imagine if Mr. Davis had been elected to Congress.

I will always choose substance over style. It is the purpose and quality of my life that matter most.

TOLERANCE

When white Americans begin to pat themselves on the back for their racial tolerance, they are getting farther away from the ideology of democracy. Tolerance is one of the finest of human virtues. There is no question. The more tolerant people become the more advanced will be the way of life of mankind. Let us have and practice tolerance to the highest degree. But let us do it quietly and from the heart. After all, tolerance is not a noisy virtue. Tolerance is the disposition to tolerate beliefs, practices, habits, and peoples of appearances differing from one's own. Let us have all of tolerance. It is by tolerance that the ideology of democracy may be made to work. But let us not substitute tolerance for democracy. Democracy is not tolerance. Democracy is a prescribed way of life erected on the premise that all men are created equal. And though it depends on tolerance to function, it is the democracy and not the tolerance which maintains that all men are created equal.

—Chester Himes,[6] 1944

REFLECTION: It would be a strange and somewhat terrifying world if every human being on earth were exactly the same. It is the diversity of our planet's residents that gives it the richness we love. Tolerance means understanding the importance of the differences in our viewpoints, lifestyles, and customs.

We do not have to agree with everything we see, hear, or read. However, we should be able to listen to people who have ideas different from our own. Tolerance permits a sharing of divergent views that often fosters growth. It allows us to accept vast differences in the beliefs and attitudes of others without making them our own. It also permits us to shed outmoded habits and perspectives in exchange for meaningful new ones. In our rapidly changing world, tolerance is a rare commodity in great demand. Being tolerant allows us to stop judging others and move toward a true democracy that benefits us all.

Practice tolerance. It is a gift that blesses both the receiver and the giver.

MISTAKES

Like a child, I had always believed that nothing was impossible until it could be proven impossible. I had optimism to the Nth degree. Pessimism is unfortunately for the sick of mind, for those who have complexes. I have found that all human beings have limitations, which is something everyone should take into consideration. We should recognize that everybody is capable of making a mistake, and we should not raise any more hell about somebody else's mistake than we expect to be raised when we make one. Who does not make mistakes? Who is not limited? Everybody but God.

—Duke Ellington,[7] 1973

REFLECTION: Duke Ellington's wise words come from fifty years of leading the Ellington band, an assemblage of extremely talented eccentrics who were cutups off the bandstand. Duke continually forgave them the errors of their ways and mistakes of judgment. All he asked was that they perform to the best of their abilities when they were onstage. More than most people, he understood the human desire to live life to the fullest. All of us make mistakes, Duke would say. Let it go. Only the Creator is perfect.

When I make another mistake, I will carry a new understanding for humanness in my heart. I will treat others the way I hope to be treated.

BLACK SOLIDARITY

We talk so much about black unity, but some of the same people crying black togetherness seem to create ways to keep us divided and fragmented. Sometimes it appears that we should worry more about how we split among ourselves and less about how whites keep us divided. We have to give up the narrow individualistic approach so that the brother in Harlem can relate to the brothers in Mississippi and feel that common bond. I believe the best chance for black survival lies in black solidarity, with the mental strength to deal in the affairs of the whole world.

—Dr. Alvin Poussaint,[8] 1970

REFLECTION: When you were growing up how many times did you hear "Be careful of the company you keep"? Or, as my grandfather loved to say: "Contamination by association." One always likes to think that all of the Black people you meet will be positive, and will encourage you to do something with your life. My elders pointed out those who were doing nothing with their lives but were always eager to backbite those who were trying to achieve their goals. Those naysayers bad-mouthed anyone who accomplished something, dismissing them as Uncle Toms, or sellouts who compromised to receive preferential treatment. You'd hear: "Since he's got a little position, he's started acting white."

It is time for all of us to steer clear of those who seek to divide and conquer Black people from within. Such malcontents are dangerous company. We must learn to seek out those who are committed to solidifying our common bond, our sense of unity. We no longer have the luxury of focusing on what white people don't do; we must focus on what Black people can do now.

Black solidarity is the foundation for the progress of our people.

SHARING THE WEALTH

The most important thing, however, is not how big you become or how much money you make. The important thing is what you do with the money you have. I was at a school recently and was introduced with a flourish as an authentic millionaire. I got up and told the students to study hard so they could contribute something to the world. As I was leaving, a boy came up to me and asked for my autograph. He said he was proud of me and he added: "I want to get a Cadillac like you." I got the impression that that was all money meant to that boy. That was his image. I decided that day to stop driving Cadillacs. A Cadillac is no evidence of having arrived; too often it is evidence of bad judgment.

Money is no good unless it contributes something to the community, unless it builds a bridge to a better life. Any man can make money, but it takes a special kind of man to use it responsibly.

—A. G. Gaston,[9] 1975

REFLECTION: A popular Black magazine ran a feature story about a wealthy entertainer who possesses three homes and a wardrobe large enough to supply a clothing store. The article concerned the loss of his prized collection of eighteen cars in a Malibu mudslide. The star said he was inconsolable and that it would take some time for him to recover. Perhaps the loss of his prized cars was a message from the Creator.

If we are blessed with a life of prosperity, it is imperative that we do not define the value of our lives by our ability to accumulate more things. It's not about getting good publicity. It's about doing the right thing. A. G. Gaston, a successful Black businessman, used his wealth to finance progressive political causes such as the Civil Rights Movement. As Gaston's life demonstrates, money spent solely on ourselves has little value. It is only when it is shared with others that money fulfills its true purpose.

My money, like my time, is a treasure to be shared.

LOVING THE TRUTH

Any time you catch folks lying, they are skeered of something. Lying is dodging. People with guts don't lie. They tell the truth and then if they have to, they fight it out. You lay yourself open by lying. The other fellow knows right off that you are skeered of him and he's more'n apt to tackle you. If he don't do nothing, he starts to looking down on you from then on. Truth is a letter from courage. I want you to grow guts as you go along. So don't you let me hear of you lying. You'll get 'long all right if you do like I tell you. Nothing can't lick you if you never get skeered.

—Zora Neale Hurston,[10] 1942

REFLECTION: Have you ever been caught in a lie? Then you know that whenever you tell a lie, you're only creating more work for yourself. Lying may sometimes seem like the easy way out, but it holds us fast in a sticky web, tangling us up until maintaining the lie becomes a full-time job. We've all been scared and we've all told a lie at some point—to get a job, to hurt someone's reputation, to break up a romance, to save ourselves from the truth.

Ultimately, though, the lie ends up hurting us more than the truth ever could. In the end, the truth is easier.

Today I must love truth. With honesty, there is nothing I cannot face.

HONEST ACHIEVEMENT

Who are we today, and where should we be going? No clear answers to these questions come from the black institutions of yesteryear. Now television, that is to say, America, has taken over the education of our young people, so that where blacks once spoke, as corny as it was, of "racial uplift," we now speak of "getting over." But this is an amoral concept. One gets over any way one can. Thus a curious inversion has taken place. The method now used to combat (make it, survive) in America is no longer ours, but America's own: unscrupulousness. But once one starts down that road, it cannot be contained within black/white relations alone. Lack of principles seeps over into our own cultural space, contaminating and poisoning relations which must be solid and honest to ensure the legitimate preservation—not to mention the prevailing—of the race.

—William Strickland,[11] *1979*

REFLECTION: "Getting over" has become the number one measure of success in some parts of the African American community. Some con artists boast that "work is for chumps." They prefer clever schemes that, with a minimum of effort, separate others from what is legally theirs. To these players, punching a time clock, playing by the rules, and making your word your bond is a sucker's game.

Those who specialize in unscrupulous smooth talk use their charms to violate every societal rule. They expertly separate the unsuspecting from their time, their money, and their common sense. The trick is, they contend, to never have to deliver on their promises.

"Getting over" flies in the face of traditional African American values, the values that have guaranteed black survival in this country for over three hundred years. If "getting over" means that we have cheated, manipulated, or maliciously hurt others—then just how far did we get?

What I've achieved doesn't matter nearly as much as how I attained the prize.

HIGH STANDARDS

I'll tell you something else that annoyed me. When they opened my locker, everybody was surprised at how neat it was. They thought Negroes were dirty, sloppy people, but my locker was perfectly clean and neat, and my one uniform—the only one I could afford—was scrubbed, starched, and ironed. The other girls' lockers were pigsties. And the Dean said, "Look at Miss Delany's locker! It is an example to you all."

You see, when you are colored, everyone is always looking for your faults. If you are going to make it, you have to be entirely honest, clean, brilliant, and so on. Because if you slip up once, the white folks say to each other, "See, what'd I tell you." So you don't have to be as good as white people, you have to be better or the best. When Negroes are average, they fail, unless they are very, very lucky. Now, if you're average and white, honey, you can go far. Just look at that Dan Quayle. If that boy was colored, he'd be washing dishes somewhere.

There are plenty of white folks who say, "Why haven't Negroes gotten further than they have?" They say about Negroes, "What's wrong with them?" To those white people, I have this to say: Are you kidding?

—A. Elizabeth Delany of The Delany Sisters,[12] 1994

REFLECTION: Uncle Russell was always telling me how important it was not to let ourselves be defined solely by race. He emphasized that we should not be disheartened when less skilled whites were promoted over more talented Blacks. He taught me that we must be unfailingly committed to ourselves.

This commitment must come from within, not from without. Some of us quit if what we want doesn't come immediately. Well, if it doesn't come today, get up and try again tomorrow! If you're facing discrimination in the workplace, or in school, and it's impeding your progress—confront it directly, but sanely!

Shut out the whispers and the shouts of those who say you cannot achieve. Be steady and persistent. Set the standard for your own life. Real commitment to higher standards in your life requires a total merging of word and deed, thought and action. Commit to yourself!

I will not be deterred from my goals by those who expect nothing from me. I will remain committed to my own high standards.

HELPING OTHERS

Am I my brother's keeper? I have to be. The poor people, who live just above the welfare and relief, have to live by that old saying, "I can see farther over the mountain than the man who is standing atop of it." We know and see the problems, because we have to live so close to them. We know that we have a sense of responsibility, and we (some of us) have tried to instill some of the ambitions we could not realize into our children. . . .

. . . Middle class and rich people take things for granted, things that we would call heaven, your nice painted walls, for instance, while we, as I heard a little boy say, "Lay down in bed at night, look through the ceiling and see shooting stars." You have your nice wall to wall carpets, while we have our little 9 by 12 linoleums that will not cover half of the floor, and will wear out before long because of the awful floors that they cover.

Am I my brother's keeper? I have to be. . . . These are the people who will be able to send their children to colleges, who will be able to pay their bills, buy their homes. . . . These are the people who want to and will get a little respect. This is why I am, why I have to be my brother's keeper.

—Helen Howard,[13] 1965

REFLECTION: How often do we think: Am I my brother's keeper? Why should I care what happens to someone else? I've got mine, let them get their own.

Often, when things become better for us, we forget what it was like when life was hard and a constant struggle. We find new friends, new surroundings, new goals. We move away from the old neighborhoods, from our old ties to others, from our past. And yet, no matter how hard we try, we never really leave those things that far behind us. No matter how much money we make, no matter how beautiful our home or car, our past—and the sobering reality that there are those among us who need our help—still exists.

If each of us who has achieved something in our life would reach back and help someone else, we would be stronger as individuals and as a race. We have that responsibility. We only hurt ourselves when we turn our back on our own. Make a difference in someone's life. We must be our brother's and sister's keeper.

I honor my responsibility to others. I am my brother's keeper.

LIVING THE DREAM

As I sat in Chicago's Museum of Science and Industry, listening to the citations, I had a sudden and unbelievable vision of the great names entombed in this Business Hall of Fame, the Armours, the Rosenwalds, the Fields, marching in the same procession with a black boy who had walked barefooted in Mississippi mud and dreamed an impossible dream.

When I got up to acknowledge the award, I looked beyond the immediate audience and said to blacks, Hispanics, to Asians, to whites, to dreamers everywhere, that long shots do come in and that hard work, dedication, and perseverance will overcome almost any prejudice and open almost any door.

That was my faith then and it's my faith now.

I believe that the greater handicap the greater the triumph.

I believe that the only failure is failing to try.

I believe that black, brown, and white Americans are chained together by tradition, history, and a common market, and that what helps one group of Americans helps all Americans.

And if my life has meaning and color and truth, it is because millions of Americans, black and white, have proved to me that the Dream is still alive and well and living in America.

—John H. Johnson,[14] *1992*

REFLECTION: A life without dreams is a diminished life. Is it not our dreams that push us to become more than we are? Is it not our dreams that prompt us to spread our wings and attempt the seemingly impossible—as John H. Johnson, the publisher of *Ebony*, did?

Our dreams are God's way of showing us our many strengths and possibilities. Listening to their wisdom helps us aim for and attain personal and spiritual fulfillment. We must never let them die. We must nurture our dreams and transform them into reality. Dreams are our divine guidance to move past our present stumbling blocks into a world of unbelievable achievement.

I will use my dreams to urge me on toward my goals. I will not let my dreams die.

LAUGHTER

You have to smile twenty-four hours a day, Momma would say. If you walk through life showing the aggravation you've gone through, people will feel sorry for you, and they'll never respect you. She taught us that man has two ways out in life—laughing or crying. There's more hope in laughing. A man can fall down the stairs and lie there in such pain and horror that his own wife will collapse and faint at the sight. But if he can just hold back his pain for a minute she might be able to collect herself and call the doctor. It might mean the difference between his living to laugh again or dying there on the spot.

—Dick Gregory,[15] 1964

REFLECTION: Every day carries the potential for minor disasters and major crises. The accumulation of every setback, if taken too seriously, can quickly pile up and send you into an emotional tailspin. Laughter is the perfect antidote. Brooding over a situation never provides a realistic solution. You locked your keys in the car. You forgot to pay the phone bill. You didn't pick up the clothes from the cleaners. You missed your dentist appointment. It's not the end of the world. Laugh. It doesn't mean that you're silly or that you don't take life seriously. It only shows that you've put everything in its proper perspective.

The world belongs to those who can laugh at themselves.

Part 5

YOUTH

PASSING THE TORCH

The burden of carrying on this struggle today belongs to our young people, who must not feel that all the battles have been won. Though the problems they face may differ in number and kind from those my generation faced, American Negroes must continue to be vigilant, courageous, and persistent in the fight for full freedom and equality. My generation has opened doors with dignity, courage, and determination. It is the task of our young people to keep them open and to forge ahead.

—H. Claude Hudson,[1] 1969

REFLECTION: Today, many of our elders must surely be asking themselves what went wrong. Their lives and achievements were truly extraordinary in the worst of times. In just one generation since the Civil Rights Movement, something frightening has occurred. Much of our tradition of progress has been eroding quietly but steadily. Many of our youth have fallen into some of the worst habits of America. They believe our history has no relevance to them. They want nothing to do with the past.

This delusion that the "race thing has played out" must be replaced with a new code of conduct and perception that stresses personal achievement and racial responsibility. For the progress of our race, each generation must shoulder its share of the challenges. We must educate our young people about the importance of our past and the sacrifices which ensured our victories. We must stand with them side by side, encouraging and supporting them. We must show them that their role is vital in a history that is still being written.

I will challenge African American youth to take an active role in creating our history.

NEW OPPORTUNITIES

There was a time not too long ago when our race was limited in the areas in which we could make a contribution, but that period in our lives is now history. Doors are opening now that my contemporaries and I never dreamed would open. Our young men and women are turning to other fields besides law, teaching, medicine, the stage, and music. Of course, we still need and will always need good lawyers and doctors and teachers, but we also need to take full advantage of America's many other opportunities and encourage more and more of our young people to go into science and engineering, and into all the newer fields that are developing, such as electronics, data processing, and space technology. It gives me a nice warm feeling to note also the progress that our race is making in politics and foreign service. This is as it should be in a democracy, and I'm sure that many Negroes in these new fields will eventually replace people like me in the Hall of Fame.

—Louis Armstrong,[2] *1969*

REFLECTION: Once upon a time, the only jobs open to African Americans were positions as hired help hidden away in someone's home or, if we were lucky, workers in a post office or an auto factory. Not anymore. In our time, a Black man has walked in space while another served as Chief of Staff of our nation's armed forces, and there is a Black woman making history as a U.S. senator.

In today's world, new and great opportunities await those with the drive and determination to seize them. Now we can surpass the dreams of our parents. If we do not squander our energies, we can focus on forming strategies that will allow us to compete in any field. The problem is that many of us keep looking back on missed opportunities with longing and regret. What's past is past. We must concentrate on what lies ahead and remember that the door of opportunity opens for those persistent enough to find the key.

Today, I will seize each opportunity and use it to the fullest.

SAVING OUR CHILDREN

Sanity suggests that the street child learns that which prepares him to live in a world that is immediate, that is real. To fail to recognize this is to expect far too much of a human being while crediting him with far too little humanity. . . .

Now, I don't know what intelligence is. But this I do know, both from life and from literature: whenever you reduce human life to two plus two equals four, the human element within the human animal says, "I don't give a damn." You can work on that basis, but the kids cannot. If you can show me how I can cling to that which is real to me, while teaching me a way into the larger society, then I will not only drop my defenses and my hostility, but I will sing your praises and I will help you to make the desert bear fruit.

—*Ralph Ellison,*[3] *1963*

REFLECTION: A few years ago, the media coined the term "throwaway kids" to describe the hundreds of thousands of children tossed out on the streets by their parents or forced to run away because of abuse. Other young people have made their own families of gangs or have estranged themselves by retreating into the hip-hop culture. Many in our older generation are put off by the throbbing, angry, anti-establishment cop-killer lyrics of hip-hop and street rap music.

There was a time in our history when deserting our children would have been unthinkable. But now these young people are compelled to survive by any means necessary on the street—even if it means killing one another. We're actually afraid of them now—and for good reason. We abandoned them when they needed us most.

Even when our youth fail to live up to our expectations, we must keep reaching out to them. We cannot afford to lose any more of our young people.

MAKING TIME

I am particularly distressed when I hear successful adults look at children living in the inner cities and say, "Nothing can be done for them, because they are incapable of imagining anything other than the circumstances into which they were born and in which they have thus far grown up." No one knows what great things the young black child can accomplish, the one who watches you as you speed by in your car. No one can measure the loss of vision and achievement and wealth when you multiply that one child by the millions you don't see.

As I encounter these tragic young faces all over the country, I remember the faces of my brothers and sisters and cousins a half century ago, working in the fields of rural Alabama, glistening in the hot summer sun. The faces I recall are not as bitter and hopeless as the ones I see today, if only because my father and the other adults in my family understood that economic independence, our ultimate freedom and salvation, was achievable.

—Ralph Abernathy,[4] 1989

REFLECTION: In Charles Fuller's excellent play *Zooman and the Sign*, a young teenage boy who accidentally kills a small girl says: "If you treat me like an animal, I'll act like an animal." Today, too many young African Americans are following the play's axiom.

Our youth didn't always act like this. Today, young people are employing a lot of false bravado and empty words to try to make a place for themselves in this cynical world. In many cases, they have no models for acting like responsible adults.

How to save our youth is a difficult question and yet the answer is obvious. We cannot shun or neglect them. We can no longer ignore their problems and their pain. Every year thousands of them continue to cry out—"Can you help me?" Yet, when they ask for guidance many of us adults say, "No, I don't have the time."

We must make the time. Our assistance at this pivotal moment in their lives could make all the difference in the world.

How I choose to interact with our young people can make a tremendous difference in their lives—and my own!

AFRICAN AMERICAN GIRLS

The influence that we have over the male sex demands, that our minds should be instructed and improved with the principles of education and religion, in order that this influence should be properly directed. Ignorant ourselves, how can we be expected to form the minds of our youth, and conduct them in the paths of knowledge? There is a great responsibility resting somewhere, and it is time for us to be up and doing. I would address myself to all mothers, and say to them, that while it is necessary to possess a knowledge of cookery, and the various mysteries of pudding-making, something more is requisite. It is their bounden duty to store their daughters' minds with useful learning. They should be made to devote their leisure time to reading books, whence they would derive valuable information, which could never be taken from them.

—Matilda,[5] 1827

REFLECTION: Today in our patriarchal society, we often neglect to give our young African American girls the emotional and educational supports they need to thrive and succeed. This is especially important since they labor under the double burden of being both Black and female. Writing in an era when a young girl could only expect a life of cooking, cleaning, and parenting, Matilda's statement was incredibly courageous.

Today, by failing to support educational opportunities for our young girls, we condemn them to endure lives of diminished quality and shattered dreams. They are every bit as worthy of our care as our young men. It is imperative that we give our young women whatever they need to grow. There are so many professions now opening to our girls, they need our continual guidance. When the prospects of one of our young girls is diminished, the future of another Black family is threatened.

Each day I will support and encourage African American girls in the fulfillment of their dreams.

BEYOND FEAR

Fear is a wearying state. It soon brings on moral fatigue; and when it cannot resolve itself in constructive, restorative activity, it resigns a person to hostility. America pays a very heavy price for this hostility that it has permitted to congeal in the hearts of the rejected young Negroes. Persons incapable of empathizing with these rejected youngsters say all kinds of silly, irresponsible things about them. They want to attribute their condition to some congenital bestiality about the black people of the world or some inexplicable, psychopathic malady. There is too much evidence on the other side to show that those Negroes whose lives were fed and nurtured by other influences have managed to cope with America's opportunities and challenges successfully without the burden of antiwhite hatreds. Just as the correlation between crime and lack of opportunity is overwhelmingly evident, only the most naïve observers attach a racial cause to chronic hostile behavior. It is the result of rejection and fear.

—Samuel Proctor,[6] 1966

REFLECTION: Although we often witness the bravado and hostility of the young, we fail to recognize the deep fear that fuels much of their antisocial behavior. These young people have never been allowed to be kids; they have neither been wanted nor loved. They are afraid that they will be rejected if they reach out. They are afraid that they will be ridiculed or belittled if they show just how vulnerable they are. For many, fear is the dominant emotion in their lives. To help them, we must recognize the powerful grip fear has on their psyche. We must aid them in understanding how fear can fill your heart with dread, make you distrust your strengths and freeze you in place. We must teach them not to let fear control them. We must teach them not to overreact or to act impulsively.

Today, I will assist a young person in confronting their fears.

LIVES TRANSFORMED

I look forward also to the blessings of being able, through the simple elements of my own example, to turn around the lives of young people who were like me at nineteen years of age, without a bridge over troubled water, with no one to turn to, and with a disbelief in themselves. I hope that my example will allow them to say, "If you could overcome all of that so can I." I will remind them that "it's not so much about where you live, it's what's living in you." If we do nothing else as an organization, we must find a way to convey that to all young people in this country, regardless of their race or religion, to tell them that the future that we care so much about is a future that really belongs to them, and that they one day must become caretakers if we are to make America the nation that it should and must be.

—Congressman Kweisi Mfume,[7] 1995

REFLECTION: Lives such as those of Maya Angelou, Malcolm X, and Congressman Mfume have great meaning for us because they show us that anyone can turn their life around and become an influential contributor to the Black community. No matter what setback or cruel twist of fate, we always have a chance to change our lives for the better. Even when all hope has been lost, there is still reason to try to redeem one's life.

If we want our young people to believe in the promises of democracy and America, we must help them see that it's possible to rise from the ashes and achieve a position of influence and affluence, locally or nationally. Only through the struggles and achievements of those who went before can our youth see that another route is possible. Through the stories of our elders they can learn why it's so important that we never give up, never sink to our knees and quit. As long as we try, there is hope and the possibility of a brighter tomorrow for ourselves and for our future generations.

I will let the example of my transformed life serve as a beacon for our lost youth.

WHAT MONEY CAN'T BUY

America is a country that makes you want things, but doesn't give you the means to get those things. Little Black children sit in front of the t.v. set and all they see are fine cars, perfumes, clothes and everything else they ain't got. They sit there and watch it, telling the rats to sit down and stop blocking their view. Ain't nobody told them, though, that they don't have any way of getting any of that stuff. They couldn't even get full at supper, but that don't matter.

—H. Rap Brown,[8] 1969

REFLECTION: Just two years ago, the poorest of our youth were killing each other over designer clothes and trinkets. Such consumer madness highlights a terrible lack of self-esteem among our youth, who are willing to separate someone from their life for a pair of Air Jordans. Their actions are dictated by a lust for possessions—just as much as many middle-class Blacks who strive to acquire more than they need. For these youths, theft is often the only way they can get what they want. They've been locked out of a system that denies them an adequate education or a decent job.

Consumerism plagues and erodes the morality of our communities. What our youth do not understand is that these things they desire most will soon go out of style and become worthless. They don't see that TV and glossy magazines seduce them into wanting things that add nothing of substance to their lives. We must teach our young people to find worth in themselves, not in what they fill their homes with or put on their backs.

I have the courage not to be a slave to my possessions.

THINKING FOR OURSELVES

One of the first things I think young people, especially nowadays, should learn is how to see for yourself and listen for yourself and think for yourself. Then you can come to an intelligent decision for yourself. If you form the habit of going by what you hear others say about someone, or going by what others think about someone, instead of searching that thing out for yourself and seeing for yourself, you will be walking west when you think you're going east, and you will be walking east when you think you're going west. This generation, especially of our people, has a burden, more so than any other time in history. The most important thing that we can learn to do today is to think for ourselves.

—Malcolm X,[9] 1964

REFLECTION: The odds of survival for our young people will greatly improve as they learn to think for themselves. Without the ability to think for ourselves, we can fall prey to anyone's or anything's influence. By thinking for ourselves, we are better equipped to handle the sudden turbulence of discord and change in our lives. By thinking intelligently and clearly and independently, we spend less time reacting to the actions of others. By thinking for ourselves, we make the appropriate choices for our lives, choices for our own best interests.

Daily, we encounter endless opportunities to make reasonable, rational choices for ourselves. It is only by clear, insightful thinking that we can dignify ourselves as men and women through our choices. These choices determine who we are and who we become. Malcolm X often said that we are truly free when we can think for ourselves. We are truly free when we are no longer preoccupied with what others think. It is up to us, as their parents and friends, to encourage our youth to develop intellectually and morally. It is one of the best gifts we can give our youth.

I will encourage our young people to think for themselves, to find their own way, to sing their own song.

Part 6

EDUCATION

THE MORE YOU LEARN

Not one of us—black or white—knows how to walk when we get here. Not one of us knows how to open a window, unlock a door. Not one of us can master a staircase. We are absolutely ignorant of the almost certain results of falling out of a five-story window. None of us comes here knowing enough not to play with fire. Nor can one of us drive a tank, fly a jet, hurl a bomb, or plant a tree.

We must be taught all that. We have to learn all that. The irreducible price of learning is realizing that you do not know. One may go further and point out—as any scientist, or artist, will tell you—that the more you learn, the less you know; but that means that you have begun to accept, and are even able to rejoice in, the relentless conundrum of your life.

—James Baldwin,[1] 1980

REFLECTION: We should never be afraid to admit what we do not know. Once we can do this, we're on the path to true knowledge. Sometimes learning comes after relentless questioning. Sometimes it comes after a string of terrible errors. Nevertheless, all of our lessons are important; we cannot ignore them. It's up to us to use them in our lives.

For most of us, it takes time to understand and digest what we've learned. And if we don't catch on, life will keep presenting us with the same challenges until we get it right.

When we open ourselves up to the wonders of learning, we discover that our potential for growth has no bounds, and with this knowledge comes the foresight and courage to make new and better choices. As we continue to learn, we expand and enrich our lives.

I've learned that there is always more in life to learn.

GOOD MEDICINE

The American Negro must remake his past in order to make his future. Though it is orthodox to think of America as the one country where it is unnecessary to have a past, what is a luxury for the nation as a whole becomes a prime social necessity for the Negro. For him, a group tradition must supply compensation for persecution, and pride of race the antidote for prejudice. History must restore what slavery took away, for it is the social damage of slavery that the present generation must repair and offset.

—Arthur A. Schomburg,[2] 1925

REFLECTION: There are people who wish our past would go away. They say we dwell too much on its agonies. They point out that slavery was as much the work of Blacks as it was of whites, adding that this bit of history is often ignored so that the issue of bondage can be falsely politicized by demagogues.

Columnist Thomas Sowell recently attacked Black teachers of Afrocentric history for "creating a phony history and phony traditions as escapes from the very real problems of drugs, violence, and social degeneration in the ghettos of the 1990s."

However, what Sowell and others fail to understand is that many of the problems now affecting the inner city stem from our young people's powerful feelings of not being connected to anybody or anything. Nowhere can they find images that consistently affirm their worth. A positive self-image rooted in an admittedly politicized past can offer many lessons of strength, healing, and perseverance. As Schomburg urged, such lessons can be used to repair and offset much of the current negative social damage heaped upon us.

Learning the truths of our pasts is good medicine for what ails us.

BRAINPOWER

Black people in this country face a grueling challenge of survival. Many of the most powerful forces in the land are arrayed against us these days, some openly and some secretly. So we need to put down all the nonsense and bull, and get about the business of manning the ramparts. . . .

Let's face reality: we don't have enough firepower to take this country; we don't have enough manpower to dominate it; we don't have enough dollar-power to buy it. And we'll be short of all these "powers" until we develop a lot more brainpower.

—Carl T. Rowan,[3] 1973

REFLECTION: Historically, education has been our ticket to a better life. The slave owners understood the power of a mind sparked by knowledge, and considered it dangerous. For this reason, slaves were forbidden the gifts of reading and education. Once that restriction was lifted, others were imposed such as separate but unequal schools and, later, substandard inner-city schools.

In the 1960s, community activists knew that they had to push for a constructive curriculum in the classroom. Still, that emphasis on core educational issues failed to increase college enrollment in our community. Too many of us did not continue our educational quest after high school. This brain drain has hampered our fight for parity in the American workplace. We need to pursue lifelong learning so that our collective brainpower will be of continued benefit to our community.

Education is a tool for transforming and revitalizing my life. With it, all dreams and goals are possible.

LEARNING

I know most of you can't spell your name. You don't know the alphabet, you don't know how to read, you don't know homonyms or how to syllabicate. I promise you that you will. None of you has ever failed. School may have failed you. Well, goodbye to failure, children. Welcome to success. You will read hard books in here and understand what you read. You will write every day so that writing becomes second nature to you. You will memorize a poem every week so that you can train your minds to remember things. It is useless for you to learn something in school if you are not going to remember it.

But you must help me to help you. If you don't give anything, don't expect anything. Success is not coming to you, you must come to it.

—Marva Collins,[4] *1982*

REFLECTION: The joy of teaching comes from planting seeds of competence in previously unfurrowed soil. Marva Collins, one of America's most gifted teachers, is also one of our most talented motivators. With good reason, she values the "wonder of learning" as a highly effective tool for our advancement, both individually and collectively. She believes that there is a world full of new discoveries and experiences awaiting each and every one of us if we will just cast off our self-imposed rigid limitations.

We often act as though we know everything when, in fact, we know so little. In a constantly evolving world, being able to learn and grow is our greatest challenge. The true quest for knowledge is never a waste of time and energy. Learning helps us grow. It frees our creative gifts. It helps us mature spiritually, and to understand life's mysteries. Open your mind to the wonders of learning, and its rewards.

Today, I will revitalize my mind and my life through the joy and wonder of learning.

TELEVISION

I absolutely forbid television to my children Monday through Friday because I found that they did not know how to talk to each other. They weren't developing themselves or listening to other people. If you don't learn how to develop your mind, body and learn how to communicate, then you are inferior. What television does is to help us to maintain an individuality that is self-destructive. That in itself is enough to determine how technology plays a part on us.

—Dr. Fletcher Robinson,[5] 1977

REFLECTION: When I was five years old, I saw a television commercial for a miniature scuba diver that I desperately wanted. My father explained that the action toy probably was nothing like what the commercial promised. I pestered him for the diver for weeks until he finally bought it. When I saw the toy, I was devastated. It was much smaller than the advertised product and its arms and legs didn't move. I was heartbroken.

None of us in America has enjoyed the same relationship with "reality" since television was introduced nationwide in 1951. The influence of television weighs heavily on the Black community. Researchers have found that while parents watch TV for entertainment, children use it for information about the world. A lot of false information comes out of our television sets.

Although television can be informative and educational, it can also be a barrier to developing and enjoying the arts of thinking and communicating. We must take responsibility for how much television we watch and what type of programs our families view.

Television is a tool that must be used wisely. I must monitor the images I allow it to project in my home.

READING

I was a young girl. I worked in a bag-making factory in town. I worked on a machine. They would come around to see if I was in school. It wasn't bad work. Young kids got good opportunities now. In the South, a lot of colored valued education then, but the white folks didn't want you to have it. In the old days, in my mother's time, I heard colored people had to pray in secret and learn to read in secret. The white man didn't want us to learn. My mother went to school with Uncle Moses. Colored taught each other then. A book was a precious thing. If they knew something, then they passed it on to someone else. We got a good foundation.

—Rose Smith,[6] 1971

REFLECTION: Almost before I could run as a small child, my grandmother Rose Smith and my great-grandmother Ida Hollingshead taught me my alphabet. They continually emphasized reading, knowledge, and school, reminding me repeatedly that reading was once a crime for Black people punishable by law. These two women convinced me at a very young age that reading was an essential skill for progress in life.

Today, reading is no longer a valued commodity in African American life. Our communication skills suffer because of our unwillingness to make reading a priority in our lives. We must learn to read effectively! A mastery of reading opens entire worlds. It also guarantees an abundance of job opportunities and life possibilities.

You can read well, so why not volunteer to teach others. Help others open their minds. Read.

Reading is critical to our growth and survival as a people.

VALUE OF EDUCATION

Education being an object of the highest importance to the welfare of society, we shall endeavour to present just and adequate views of it, and to urge upon our brethren the necessity and expediency of training their children, while young, to habits of industry, and thus forming them for becoming useful members of society. It is surely time that we should awake from this lethargy of years, and make a concentrated effort for the education of our youth. We form a spoke in the human wheel, and it is necessary that we should understand our pendence on the different parts, and theirs on us, in order to perform our part with propriety.

—Samuel Cornish and John B. Russwurm,[7] 1827

REFLECTION: Do you read to your children every night? Do you go over their homework with them? Do you know the names of their teachers or the courses they are taking? Do you monitor what they watch on television?

If your answer is "no" to any of these questions, it's time to make a change. We must continually stress the importance of education in the lives of our children. Education is not "a white thing." It's an essential tool for survival and success in this modern, high-tech world.

Life can never overwhelm our children if ignorance is no longer a part of their curriculum. Today, I will devote more time to the education of my child.

TRY SOMETHING NEW

Experimentation and development work hand in hand toward progress. Effective advances are made daily because new things are tried and occasionally they are successful. The refusal to venture out in the unknown, to only use one way, to remain constant and sometimes stagnate, is certainly defeatist in terms of an ideology of education for oppressed people. We must view failure as a reward for having come forth and tried to do something new. For having assumed your manhood and tried to take things into your own hands, you have experienced failure. We must understand to that end, failure is not irrevocable. Free men have failed today, only to experience overwhelming success on the next try.

—Jitu Weusi,[8] 1974

REFLECTION: All of us are afraid of failure. For many of us, that fear keeps us from progressing in life. *Black Enterprise* publisher Earl G. Graves once remarked that "failure is not a fatal disease." In fact, it is our failures that shape our successes and give them a deeper meaning.

There is no such thing as absolute success or absolute failure. Even in the greatest achievement, there is the tiniest seed of something that you know you could have done better, something that you wish you could have changed. Still, that does not diminish the sweetness of your success. To move forward, we need to be willing to fail. Never let fear of failure stop you from trying something new in your life. If you fall on your face, remember there's always next time.

Playing it safe only leads to stagnation. Failure will not kill us, but mediocrity can.

OPPORTUNITY

If we want something out of life, we've got to realize that we must give something of ourselves. If we expect to get good jobs, we have to accept the fact that we must first qualify for them. We shouldn't expect to be given an opportunity, or a job, or a position merely because we're Negroes. The most important thing that I try to stress in my work is that we must qualify ourselves for the opportunities that exist or that will come. If we're qualified and then are turned down in any respect, we may be disturbed or feel disgusted, but we shouldn't let the way we feel change our outlook on life. You know, I said earlier that regardless of what profession a person might choose—or whether he's white or black—if he believes in himself, if he knows he has the ability, and if he has faith, no one can stop him. The whole world can't stop a determined man!

—Jersey Joe Walcott,[9] 1969

REFLECTION: Like any other race, we have our share of the lazy, the unenthused, and the ill-prepared—people who expect to get something for nothing and expect the rewards of life to come without any sweat or sacrifice. They're the first to complain that they're not being given a free ride. Opportunities sometimes come unexpectedly, but for the most part, they have to be earned.

One day, the critically acclaimed actor Morgan Freeman was asked how it felt to be an overnight sensation. He smiled patiently and answered that he was an overnight sensation that was fifteen years in the making. His opportunity presented itself only after years of arduous training and unsung work in small theaters. Freeman qualified himself long before the spotlight turned in his direction. He was ready to seize his moment when his golden opportunity came.

When opportunity knocks, I will be prepared to welcome it in.

Part 7

FAMILY

LOVING SUPPORT

The real source of Black strength has been Black Love. The sense of Blackness or Black love has, in turn, been the impetus for Black families to ensure our survival. Most of us can recall the special warmth (regardless of white research findings) which characterized our families and, most of us, if honest, also see that our success and survival depended on the family from which we came. It gave us strength and commitment to struggle to succeed. It also instilled in us a special appreciation for the "collective well-being" of all Black people.

—Dr. Wade Nobles,[1] 1978

REFLECTION: Activist and entertainer Paul Robeson credited the "comfort and support" of his family for providing him with the emotional and spiritual power he needed to attain his lofty achievements. His family, he added, also gave him the tools to weather all of the extreme challenges he faced in his life.

Nothing can substitute for the feeling of being appreciated and valued by your own blood relations. The affirmation and nourishment derived from one's family makes even the most feeble spirit robust. Remember your father's big smile of pride when you got your high school diploma or took high honors when you graduated from college? Remember your mother's happiness when you landed a big promotion at your job?

How many of us take the blessing of a supportive, caring family for granted? If you have problems communicating with your family, seek out new ways to resolve your disagreements and rediscover your common ground. Cherish your family as your most vital resource.

I'm finding new ways to show my love, respect, and gratitude for the loving support of family.

BLACK MOTHERS

The Negro mother has had the bitter job of teaching her children the difference between the White and Colored signs before they are old enough to attend school. She had to train her sons and daughters to say "sir" and "ma'am" to those who were their sworn enemies.

She couldn't tell her husband "a white man whistled at me, or insulted me, or touched me," not unless she wanted him to lay down his life before organized killers who strike only in anonymous numbers. Or worse, perhaps to see him helpless and ashamed before her.

Because he could offer no protection or security, the Negro woman has worked with and for her family. She built churches, schools, temples, and college educations out of soapsuds and muscle.

—Alice Childress,[2] 1966

REFLECTION: No amount of gratitude can repay our debt to the African American mother. She has stayed the course through times both good and bad—always keeping her eye on the prize. She has made endless sacrifices to preserve the black family. Her selflessness for our people is legendary. Without much acclaim or praise, she has often served as the moral compass for our race.

Understanding the demands of the white world, the African American mother acted as the mediator between her children and an often hostile environment. When a biased society sought to demean and humiliate her man, she became his buffer, his counsel, his comfort. We cannot measure the worth of what she has done to keep us alive and defiant as a people. When we consider our mothers' historic contribution to the Black community, we realize that no praise is too great.

No gift of love, support, or recognition is big enough for my mother.

PARENTHOOD

The mothers and fathers and the men and women of our race must often pause and ask: Is it worth while?

Ought children be born to us?

Have we a right to make human souls face what we face today?

The answer is clear: if the great battle of human right against poverty, against disease, against color prejudice is to be won, it must be won not in our day, but in the day of our children's children. Ours is the blood and dust of battle, theirs the rewards of victory. If then they are not there because we have not brought them to the world, then we have been the guiltiest factor in conquering ourselves.

—W. E. B. Du Bois,[3] 1912

REFLECTION: Parenthood is an honor which celebrates the cycles of life. It requires great courage and daring. It compels each and every man and woman who takes on this role to face himself or herself in ways that can be avoided when one is alone and self-absorbed. Many of us forgo parenthood because we're terrified to look deeply into our hearts to assess how much love we can give. But we must remember that in addition to the awesome responsibility, parenthood brings tremendous joy.

Parenthood is the satisfaction we feel when we see our children using the values and skills we've taught them. It fills us with pride to watch our children become secure in themselves, formulate goals, and stretch their wings beyond the boundaries of home. It is a pleasure to watch our children make their unique and invaluable contributions to our community. Parenthood is the true affirmation of our family history and our collective history as a people.

I have the vision and courage to bring new life into the world. Our children are our offering to our ancestors and our gift to the future of our race.

BLACK FAMILY

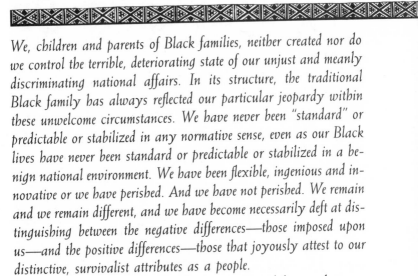

We, children and parents of Black families, neither created nor do we control the terrible, deteriorating state of our unjust and meanly discriminating national affairs. In its structure, the traditional Black family has always reflected our particular jeopardy within these unwelcome circumstances. We have never been "standard" or predictable or stabilized in any normative sense, even as our Black lives have never been standard or predictable or stabilized in a benign national environment. We have been flexible, ingenious and innovative or we have perished. And we have not perished. We remain and we remain different, and we have become necessarily deft at distinguishing between the negative differences—those imposed upon us—and the positive differences—those that joyously attest to our distinctive, survivalist attributes as a people.

Today we must distinguish between responsibility and consequence. We are not responsible for the systematic underemployment and unemployment of Black men or women. We are not responsible for racist hatred of us, and we are not responsible for the American contempt for women per se. We are not responsible for a dominant value system that quibbles over welfare benefits for children and squanders deficit billions of dollars on American pie in the sky. But we must outlive the consequences of this inhumane, disposable-life ideology. We have no choice.

—June Jordan,[4] 1987

REFLECTION: The Black family is not dead or dying. It will adapt to the current socio-political reality as it has to the ceaseless history of challenges on these shores. June Jordan, one of our more astute cultural critics, sees resilience as the basic strength of the African American family. No matter what obstacles and situations have confronted it, the Black family has survived. Many conservatives view the single-parent family in the Black community as a sign of our decline. And certainly, there is reason for concern given the long list of societal problems afflicting a significant number of our people. However, many communities, with the support of churches and other local institutions, are working to save the embattled Black family.

We've always had single-parent families. And those families did not face moral condemnation or isolation. Yes, these are tough times, but just as the Black family survived slavery, it will survive this present crisis. We must extend the branches of our family tree to offer shelter for all against the current storm.

I will do my part to ensure the survival of the Black family.

A BETTER LIFE

So much of what we as black people are has to do directly with the fact that our forefathers were not able to pass on the good life to us. We knew that there was a good life to be had, and we knew what the passport would be—hard work. Of course, it wasn't always a guaranteed passport, but it was essential if you were to have any chance at all. With that philosophy, many black kids whose parents didn't have the means to send them to college worked their way through by busing dishes in the cafeteria, mowing lawns in town, working as maids, pumping gas, scrubbing floors, or whatever else was necessary to pay for their own educations. Black youngsters were not the only ones using the hard-work philosophy to move upward and onward—loads of white kids were doing the same thing—but to a greater extent the black youngsters' parents had to say to them: "If you want a better life—and I want a better life for you—I will help you as much as I can, but I cannot hand it to you. You are going to have to get it for yourself, for the most part, and getting it yourself requires that, first, you have an education, and, second, that you go out there and work for it." An impressive number of them did just that. The glittering list of America's most successful blacks is generously sprinkled with the names of those who pumped gas, scrubbed floors, bused dishes, and even shined shoes.

—Sidney Poitier,[5] 1980

REFLECTION: African Americans have long valued education as the key to greater achievement. No sacrifice was too great for our parents and grandparents to make for our education. When the salaries earned from their service jobs were insufficient, many parents worked two or three jobs to cover the financial burden. The legacy of their sacrifice and hard work increased the ranks of Black teachers, Black doctors, Black scientists, Black engineers, Black lawyers, and Black journalists.

Today, the commitment to Black academic and professional achievement has slackened. The numbers of Black youth attending college have significantly declined, while the importance of higher education has never been greater. Many of us believe that we should no longer be required to sacrifice anything to reach our goals. Many of us are no longer willing to work twice as hard to guarantee our success. Both sacrifice and hard work are crucial to keep Black people moving forward.

The foundation of Black achievement rests upon the bedrock of education and hard work.

FAMILY REUNIONS

I really want to make as big an impact as I can among younger black people about the vital importance of us going to our oldest people and talking with them and finding out what they know about our families. There is black history untold in the memories of the hundreds of thousands of grandmothers, grandfathers, great-aunts, great whatever. Nobody asks them.

Another thing I'd like to have a lot to do with if I can is to see if I can radically increase the number of family reunions held among black people. There is something about, something chemical that happens when a group of people with the same blood connection, blood-marriage connections, come together for the purpose of being together as such.

—Alex Haley,[6] 1976

REFLECTION: Family reunions have been a tradition among African Americans for generations. Since the 1976 publication of Alex Haley's *Roots*, the number of Black family reunions has soared to record levels. More than six million people have attended the Black family reunion weekends sponsored by the National Council of Negro Women since 1986. Hundreds of thousands of Black families come together every year to restore and strengthen their bond by gathering to discuss the prized history of the clan. The popularity of these reunions flies in the face of media pronouncements about the "disappearing Black family."

You don't need a large group to come together to nurture the family tree. An effective family reunion can involve a few members of the bloodline, or just one young member sitting down with an honored elder and tape-recording a chapter of family history. Preserving the words and remembrances of family elders for posterity is a perfect legacy for future generations. When the energy and vitality of that blood bond is released, it can rejuvenate every leaf on the family tree.

Gather the members of your family together as often as possible. Absorb the unity, strength, and history that radiate from the extended family tree.

THE GOOD FATHER

My father saves people, I often thought. People talked of what a fine social worker he was and how many young people he had helped set in the right direction. He raised money for Y scholarships, helped the young find work and provided guidance through the Y programs.

He gave fine stirring speeches at meetings and banquets on the value of working hard for the Negro cause and helping Negro youth. He read me poetry of Negro poets and told me stories of Du Bois, Marian Anderson and Mary Bethune. He listened to me sing spirituals, which I loved, and popular songs, which I also loved.

—Adrienne Kennedy,[7] 1987

REFLECTION: The Hausa tribe of West Africa affirms the importance of the role of the father in the family: "A wise father's love and words will give power and strength long after he is gone." Often the wisdom of the father is not spoken in words; rather it is communicated silently and powerfully through actions. Children watch their fathers constantly and observe how they handle life's various challenges.

The father's presence in the home is inestimable in its influence. A growing son wants to emulate a strong and loving father. A maturing daughter often chooses a man who most resembles her father, especially if he has been a positive influence in her life. Fathers must remember the importance of their example and that the work of a good father is never done. A father's love must be demonstrated through persistence, patience, strength, and understanding. African American fathers are one of the pillars of our families. Today, we acknowledge the importance of their labor of love.

I value the responsible African American fathers who invest time, energy, and love in their families and communities.

RESPECT FOR ELDERS

Dear Mama,

The things you speak of are uppermost in my mind and my heart. I am not too manly or sophisticated to say that I love you and all the rest with a devotion and dedication that will continue to grow until I pass from this existence. Anything that will please you, and that falls within human accomplishment, I will carry out. I say this with confidence because of my certainty that you would never ask me to please you by surrendering my mental liberty and self-respect; I wouldn't want to live were these, my last two real possessions, to be lost.

Any confidence you put in me, Mama, will be well placed. This is not mere talk, my ego is nowhere involved.

—George Jackson,[8] *1965*

REFLECTION: This poignant excerpt from a letter written by political firebrand George Jackson from Soledad Prison revealed a side of the man never seen by the public. Like many of us, Jackson experienced times when he disagreed with his elders. Like many of us, he asked: "What do they know?" Or: "What makes them always so right?"

Jackson, in his earlier years, had believed that the experiences of his mother were completely out of touch with the world he faced as a rebellious young man. Later, he understood his link to her world and the battles she experienced. With her love as a support, he began to redeem his life.

George Jackson grew as an individual when he realized that his mother, the woman who had given him life, only wanted him to be a man and remain true to his beliefs. It is not enough to say we love our elders. We must show them respect and deference daily in our words and actions.

Our connection with our elders is a deep and ancient one. We honor our elders most when we use their gifts to build a life filled with integrity and accomplishment.

Part 8

COMMUNITY

COMMUNITY OF LOVE

The word love is suspect; black expectations of what it might produce have been betrayed too often. But those were expectations of a response from the white community, which failed us. The love we seek to encourage is within the black community, the only American community where men call each other "brother" when they meet. We can build a community of love only where we have the ability and power to do so: among blacks.

—Kwame Touré (Stokely Carmichael),¹ 1968

REFLECTION: We know certain neighborhoods have been targeted for neglect. Garbage collection is as rare as police patrols in some sections of our communities. The roads are never repaired. Businesses have fled, leaving shuttered hulls of buildings. Only liquor stores remain, along with a smattering of overpriced markets owned by people who often live outside the neighborhoods. In this type of environment, some of us wake up every morning feeling as if someone is out to get us. It's like a war zone. And those of us who live in it are often overwhelmed with tension, paranoia, and fear. We feel nobody cares about us, so why should we care about ourselves?

What our community needs more than anything is a return to self-love and self-rule. We must love and care about ourselves and how we live because it's clear that no one else will. Who can love and respect a community that does not love and care about itself?

Where I live is as important to me as my family, job, or church. Love for my community is a priority, not an option.

GETTING INVOLVED

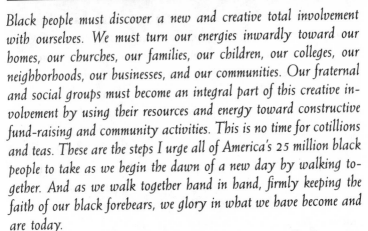

Black people must discover a new and creative total involvement with ourselves. We must turn our energies inwardly toward our homes, our churches, our families, our children, our colleges, our neighborhoods, our businesses, and our communities. Our fraternal and social groups must become an integral part of this creative involvement by using their resources and energy toward constructive fund-raising and community activities. This is no time for cotillions and teas. These are the steps I urge all of America's 25 million black people to take as we begin the dawn of a new day by walking together. And as we walk together hand in hand, firmly keeping the faith of our black forebears, we glory in what we have become and are today.

—Adam Clayton Powell, Jr.,[2] 1971

REFLECTION: We can no longer wait for the federal government to throw money at our communities like aid to a Third World nation, using the paltry scraps from the table of our own tax dollars. We must reclaim and revitalize our own communities.

We must clean up our own yards. Stop littering our own streets. Paint our own houses, and even help our neighbors paint theirs. We can no longer wait for anyone else to do this work for us. Join a church group that helps the elderly. Be a member of a crime-watch patrol. Start an after-school program for our youth. Patronize Black-owned stores in the community.

There are moral and spiritual rewards to be gained from re-investing our energies in the improvement of the lives of our families and our communities. Together, we can do more than we'd ever imagined possible.

We must learn once again to embrace the joy of doing for self. Today, I will take action to build the community where I live.

THE PROBLEMS OF LIFE

We will realize that human advance is long, slow and tedious, with periods of acceleration and stoppage, even of retrogression; undoubtedly, now and again, the world falls backward. We will realize that the inner core of the problem of American Negroes is not discrimination but a question of ideals and the emerging of ability. But the doing away with discrimination will never settle these matters— rather, it opens the way for us to face the real problems of life.

—W. E. B. Du Bois,[3] *1947*

REFLECTION: There are those of us who think that all of the problems in the African American community will end once racism and discrimination end. Not so. Several unresolved issues still remain. We will have to examine the symptoms of our internalized oppression—those problems that have nothing to do with the external society.

No one makes us rob one another. No one makes us kill one another. No one makes us steal from one another. No one makes us assault our women or abuse our children. No one makes us neglect our elders. These are internal problems that must be addressed. No one from outside of our community can do for us what we must do for ourselves. Our salvation lies in a deep, spiritual housecleaning.

God, grant me the insight, courage, and strength to truly face the problems beyond racism in my home and my community.

WELFARE

I don't dig welfare. But I can feature folk needing help to help themselves. I think it corrodes a man's or woman's integrity to get something for nothing. But I believe in incentives. The government could pay 70 percent of a poor kid's education, let's say. The government could start giving the poor some bargains—not handouts or freebies. A dollar means a hell of a lot more when you got to sweat a little blood for it.

—Ray Charles,[4] 1978

REFLECTION: Welfare is just another form of slavery. It ends up causing more problems than it solves, chaining us to an outmoded and dehumanizing system. Just think what could be done with the time spent waiting in endless lines—we could be learning new skills to make an honest living for the long haul. Let's raise our expectations.

Welfare was never supposed to be a way of life for anyone. It was mandated to help us get back up when we stumble and fall. Living on handouts wounds the soul and diminishes self-esteem. Let's create a fair exchange of resources instead of accepting help that hurts.

I will demand that my community receive the seeds of life for planting instead of settling for the half-eaten fruit.

ECONOMIC SURVIVAL

The black community now exercises little control over the $50 billion that we spend. Scant sums are channeled back into the black community and very little of it benefits these communities.

What we need now are bold strategies and staunch allies to gain control of as much of that $50 billion that passes through black hands each year as possible!

... There is more talk now of getting a piece of the action, and blacks now realize that economic development has many spinoffs.

Keeping dollars in the black community creates new jobs, makes services more accessible to the poor and the elderly, and contributes to a sense of community pride.

—*Edward W. Brooke,*[5] *1975*

REFLECTION: Long deprived of equal access to white America's passion for consumerism, African Americans saved and spent cautiously for many years, yet never bought into the acquisition of things as a solution to society's ills. They understood that money or goods didn't bring happiness, love, good health, or self-esteem.

Suddenly, in the late 1970s, Black people discovered that spending money can provide an excellent emotional release. Manufacturers and advertisers began targeting the Black market, and money began draining out of the community as never before. We no longer invest or save like our forebearers did. Too often, we buy things we don't need, forgetting that a people with no business sense often finds itself with empty pockets and a hand out for charity.

In today's economy, when money is tight for everyone, we must use our monetary resources to create a power base for ourselves. We must learn how to make our money work for us. We need to develop a clear, constructive plan for using our financial power.

Today, I will spend my hard-earned money wisely, strengthening my community in the face of an uncertain future.

JOBS

It is late for the black workers; it is late for America. Life demands an outlet, it demands something to live on. Without wages there are no means of purchasing the goods that sustain life. You can't get wages without jobs in our industrial society. Consequently, the problem of Negroes today is jobs, jobs, jobs.

Unless black workers can get jobs there is no hope for families in the Negro communities. . . .

We cannot survive unless we have something to survive on or with. This is why we must fight for jobs; we must march for jobs; we must struggle for jobs. We must sacrifice and suffer for jobs. If we are willing to do this we will get jobs. We will win this fight.

—A. Phillip Randolph,[6] *1963*

REFLECTION: The most difficult work is being out of work. If you've ever been unemployed, you understand the desperation of not knowing where your next meal will come from, or how the rent will be paid. It's all the worse if you have little ones, and their hunger is staring you in the face. A growing number of African Americans—an estimated 50 percent or more in some communities—face this challenge every day. In America, a person without a job does not live; he or she only exists. Dr. Martin Luther King, Jr., often remarked that it is all right to tell Blacks that they must lift themselves by their own bootstraps, but "it is a cruel jest to say that to a bootless man."

With safety nets such as welfare and Medicaid unraveling, the plight of the poorest of us becomes that much more urgent. We can no longer expect others to employ our young or our poor—we must look to our own, to the thousands of Black-owned businesses in this country. If you have a business of any type in our community, employ a qualified African American. If you need services performed at home or in your workplace, find a way to support one of our own.

I will reach out to create employment in my community at every level. Jobs count!

CONFRONTING VIOLENCE

Violence is accepted in America as long as it's white folks doing it. Turn on the t.v. and you go deaf from all the gunfire. Let two fighters get in the ring and let neither one of them hit the other and see what the real savages out there are going to do. They're going to scream for blood. It's no different than the people in ancient Rome who put lions on people.

—H. Rap Brown,[7] 1969

REFLECTION: The violent America that activist H. Rap Brown witnessed nearly thirty years ago was vastly different from the one now confronting us. Senseless violence has become a grim fact of life for most African Americans. We can't put all of the blame on the white man and white America.

Our children are killing each other at an alarming rate. Families—entire bloodlines—are being wiped out with more efficiency than the Ku Klux Klan could have ever mustered. Data compiled by Tuskegee University indicates that the Klan murdered 3,445 Blacks in 100 years. But that tragic figure is being dwarfed by the current estimates of nearly 8,000 Blacks being killed every single year—and over 95 percent of them by a Black finger on a trigger.

We all wring our hands over the carnage on our streets. But that isn't enough. We must change the way we're treating one another. We must begin to honor, trust, and protect one another before it's too late.

I will no longer tolerate violence in my life. Each day I will act to stop the violence in my family, in my neighborhood, and in my community.

CRIME

I don't know anyone who is for crime in the streets, or for crime anywhere else. No society can long survive if substantial numbers of people are occupied in mugging, robbing, and more high class crimes. The only trouble comes when "crime in the streets" is interpreted as meaning crimes committed by Negroes. Unfortunately, that's what many people really mean when they use the phrase. . . .

I suppose it's a mark of creeping civilization that prejudiced people talk about "crime in the streets" instead of coming right out and calling all Negroes criminals, like they did the Irish and Italians when they lived in the slums and provided a disproportionate amount of the criminals. . . . The overwhelming majority of law-abiding Negroes are being smeared by the "crime in the streets" double talk today.

But I don't want to charge anyone with prejudice, so I'll just assume that people really mean that they are against all crime.

—Whitney M. Young, Jr.,[8] 1968

REFLECTION: Crime exists throughout the world. Despite the assertions of some, crime is not the sole domain of African Americans in this country. We haven't buried children in underground prisons on our property. We haven't exploded car bombs, wreaking mass destruction on innocents.

When President Nixon spoke of "law-and-order," he spoke of us. When President Reagan spoke of "rampant crime in our cities," he spoke of us. When President Bush held up a mug shot of Willie Horton, he spoke of us. And yet, most Blacks never see the inside of a jail or go before a judge. Most African Americans are law-abiding citizens who do their best to steer clear of any interaction with police or the courts. We cannot assume the blame for the actions of those of us who choose to live lives of crime. Wrongdoing is an individual choice. Those who live by the laws of God and society must steadfastly hold their heads high. We are not a race of criminals, nor should we allow anyone to treat us as such.

We remind ourselves that criminality—the worst quality of human beings—is not the exclusive domain of Black people.

THE FORGOTTEN MAJORITY

The discussion about the underclass misses the point [because] it fails to see the connection between the classes. It's an isolated focus. The majority of African-Americans are working class, and that's where we ought to be focusing our energy. If we do a bit more to buttress the working class, people wouldn't slide into the underclass so much. In the white community, you get the middle class generating the middle class. But in the black community, the middle class is a new middle class that comes out of the working class.

The working class is the heart, the backbone, of the African-American community, yet they're ignored by the media, literature and politicians.

—Andrew Billingsley,[9] 1993

REFLECTION: Too often, we celebrate the wrong principles and the wrong people. While the outstanding accomplishments of the Black bourgeoisie and the pathologies of the Black underclass often receive the lion's share of media coverage, the fact that the majority of African Americans are working class people and the bedrock of the race goes largely unnoticed. The Black working class possesses a solid work ethic and strives to achieve the type of financial, emotional, and spiritual stability that creates a tangible legacy for the generations that follow.

Working class people have waged winning battles on many fronts—external and internal—to attain their goals. It's high time that we offer some recognition to those who have toiled without faltering. Their principles of hard work, diligence, and self-discipline are our most shining achievement.

Today, I will celebrate the significant contributions of the Black working class.

COMMUNAL SPIRIT

We have always been an African people, we have always maintained our own value system and I will prove that to you. . . .

As much as he [the whiteman] has tried, our people have resisted for 413 years in this wilderness. And they resisted for this generation to carry out what must be done. We cannot fail our ancestors, cannot fail our ancestors, cannot fail our ancestors. . . .

Check out our way of life. No matter how he's tried, we still maintain a communal way of life in our community. We do not send old people to old people's homes—that's junk. . . .

It is a level of resistance that we must begin to look for among our people. Pick up that thread and do what has to be done so that our people will survive. . . . We must first develop an undying love for our people. . . . If we do not do that, we will be wiped out.

—Kwame Touré (Stokely Carmichael),[10] 1968

REFLECTION: The African communal way of life is still with us. A few years ago, a Black farmer, living outside of Clarksdale, Mississippi, lost his child when his house burned to the ground. Traveling through the region to visit relatives, I watched as the people in his community arrived the next day with tools and lumber to build another dwelling for the man and his five remaining children. His wife wept with joy. The women served food and refreshment for the men who toiled under a blazing sun.

There was no mention of payment for the labor. For the man's neighbors, this work was done from the heart, from a deep love for one of their own who had fallen on bad times.

"We sometimes pitch a fit with each other, but by and large, we get along pretty good down here," one man told me. They were all a part of something larger, greater than themselves. There was a soul connection from each individual to the greater whole. It was a community filled and blessed with Black love.

I pay homage to my African past by honoring its revered sense of communal spirit and love.

BEYOND BLACKNESS

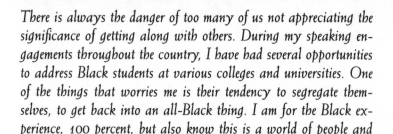

There is always the danger of too many of us not appreciating the significance of getting along with others. During my speaking engagements throughout the country, I have had several opportunities to address Black students at various colleges and universities. One of the things that worries me is their tendency to segregate themselves, to get back into an all-Black thing. I am for the Black experience, 100 percent, but also know this is a world of people and that no segment is totally independent and self-sustaining. We all depend upon each other.

We must learn a lot more before we can go off by ourselves. Every hour you deny yourself contact with your fellowman, particularly if he is different, is an hour lost in learning an experience that would not only teach you how to get along with your fellowman, but what he knows that you ought to know.

—James O. Plinton, Jr.,[11] 1974

REFLECTION: We all know people who are so afraid of the larger society, the white world, that they've stayed in the cocoon of their childhood neighborhood.

Popular wisdom once suggested that we could lose our soul if we left the Black community. People often cling to one another to shield themselves from what they see as a hostile environment outside their community. Sometimes this need for self-segregation and self-imposed isolation is validated by the example of some African American achievers who become so immersed in the larger world that they lose their sense of self and identity.

None of this can happen if you know who you are and where you have come from. Becoming successful does not have to have such a cost. There is a world of endless possibilities out there. Be a part of it. You can retain your roots, your commitment to your people, and still climb.

By venturing into the world and opening myself to all of its possibilities I can bring new wealth to my community.

THE WISDOM OF THE ELDERS

We talk a lot, these four women and I, but then we always did. They grew up hearing stories I heard from mama and aunts and the old mothers of the church. It was, it is, the way we have continued in this country, passing on our own and the wider history and culture of America. Not just of Black America, of all of it, so that we know what life was like among Black people as well as white ones during slavery time because we heard and overheard the tales of Ole Miz and what happened when. It has been, it is, our strength, this talking and listening, because we have traditionally shared not only the outward cold and definite facts, but also the inward feeling and meaning of things. It has given us knowledge that modern young women of color tend to undervalue, but it has been the knowledge that has sustained us. Young women today seem to think that one can know either the book or the bush, when in truth the full knowledge and acceptance of both is not only valuable but necessary.

—Lucille Clifton,[12] 1985

REFLECTION: Poet Lucille Clifton speaks eloquently about one of the most valuable assets in the African American community: the wisdom of our elders. They have seen and done so much, yet often their wisdom and expertise are discounted or forgotten.

We spend our time calculating how we can be smarter, richer, and more successful, while turning away from the gold mine right in our midst. We go to therapists, psychics, and hypnotists, instead of picking up the telephone to call Aunt Bessie or Uncle Silas. One day we will be asked to pass our wisdom on to those who follow us in the same way that our honored forebears once passed on their values, customs, and time-honored strengths to our generation. We cannot be the broken link in this chain. We must return to that light of wisdom that burns so brightly among us. We must draw on the nourishing warmth of our elders' presence before it is lost to us.

The knowledge I seek is often just a few steps away. Today, I will partake of the wisdom of my elders.

Part 9

RELATIONSHIPS

BLACK LOVE

A Negro man needs more, expects more, from his wife than other men do.

A Negro woman, no matter what their age or background or understanding of the problem, has to be terribly strong. They cannot relax, they cannot simply be loving wives waiting for the man of the house to come home from work. They have to be spiritual sponges, absorbing the racially inflicted hurts of their men. Yet at the same time they have to give him courage, make him know that it is worth going on, worth going back day after day to the humiliations and discouragements of trying to make it in the white man's world. It isn't easy to be a sponge and an inspiration. It doesn't leave enough room for simple love to develop. You both become victims of the system you're trying to fight. The strain on a marriage is incredible.

—Lena Horne,[1] 1965

REFLECTION: In today's high-pressure world, the stresses on the love bond between an African American man and woman are tremendous. And how many of us bring the tension we face every day in the outside world back home with us? It would be easy just to let ourselves be victims of that chaos, and let it take its toll on what we share together. But what a terrible loss that would be.

In the past, our women have worn themselves down trying to keep hearth and home together. They turned themselves inside out attempting to bring life into dying unions, while their men—angry and hurt—retreated further and further inside themselves.

What has been damaged is our link to each other. That must be restored. Our love for each other must grow and deepen in spite of the statistics that predict heartache and separation. We must have enough trust in love to reach out to each other again—to move beyond our separate pain and stand together.

Today, I will not give up on our love despite life's ups and downs. I will leave room in our relationship for simple love to grow.

HEALING LOVE

I say that love will cure everything and people say that's oversimplifying it. It's not. It's just that love will cure everything. If I love you, I don't want you hungry because it will make me feel bad. If I love you, I don't want to fight you. If I love you, I don't want to see you raggedy. If I love you, I want you to have the best of everything. So if I'm loving you, I'm not going to fight you because when I hit you, it hurts me.

—Della Reese,[2] 1982

REFLECTION: Singer Della Reese knows firsthand about the truth of her statements. In the late 1980s, the love of family and friends pulled her through a life-threatening illness and supported her in a successful comeback in her entertainment career. Many critics doubted whether she could do it. Her recovery was nothing short of miraculous.

The healing powers of love are legendary. When we feel we are deeply loved by those around us, we are transformed by that love. We are emboldened by that love to make deep, significant changes in our lives. We become more than just flesh and bone. Our internal wounds no longer bleed or fester. With love, healthy new tissue is formed and old emotional scars vanish.

Today, I will open my heart to the healing power of love.

A LIVING LOVE

One you really love is not around, but with other people. There is the possibility of being jealous. You feel that he is fonder of someone else or that he understands another one better. This is pure selfishness, a kind of love that is not, in fact, genuine. . . . What is required is the feeling of deep, deep love, the kind that wraps itself all around your insides, but does not choke you.

There are loves that choke the love that satisfies. Real love is the love that knows that whenever and wherever you meet again, it's going to be bigger than ever.

—*Pearl Bailey*,[3] *1971*

REFLECTION: Many of us are addicted to love—any kind of love. The sentimentality of romantic movies and the lyrics of love songs promote the illusion that only a love that fulfills our hidden fantasies is real. And when we find ourselves in a relationship that contains any of these false ingredients, we cling to it for dear life.

Trying to live out romantic illusions only leads to anxiety, frustration, turmoil, and jealousy. Once these penetrate a relationship, real love and tenderness begin to fade. Love must be allowed to grow freely in real time, in real life. When this happens, love only gets better and better.

Let us learn to be realistic in affairs of the heart. Let's give love a chance to breathe and grow.

INTIMACY

What have I learned? That the most special part about being with a woman is to hold them. You know, just maybe to touch their hand. To have a friend there and touch their hand at the right moment. Just that. For all the anxiety about the sexual act, it's not what it's made out to be, yet it's so much more than anything one could ever imagine. When you really care about someone. There's nothing that I know of that can touch intimacy. It's more than sex. Sex is something else, I think. But there's intimacy; you can touch someone's toes with your foot. To be that close. Or just touch someone's cheek or feel their breath on your cheek. And look in someone's eyes and know that you're looking at the truth.

—Richard Pryor,[4] 1986

REFLECTION: Before the Sexual Revolution, the rules of intimacy were simple and straightforward. Intimacy was a valued part of courtship and love. Everyone knew what was acceptable and what was not. Today, many of those rules are no longer in effect and no one seems to know what works in relationships anymore. Sex is often mistaken for intimacy. But real intimacy grows out of a caring for the other person and a deep commitment to partnership.

Intimacy is the connective tissue of love. It is the most effective antidote to breakup and divorce.

Intimacy is the touchstone of abiding love. As Richard Pryor explains, intimacy is about tenderness and a gentle expression of love—often without words. The soft caress, the easy smile, the warm glance. These wholehearted emotions speak of our total willingness to grow together, to keep faith in our bond, to expect the best from each other despite whatever obstacles may arise.

Intimacy sustains the emotional and spiritual bonds of love. It binds two hearts together, and makes them one.

DEEP LOVE

Our sharing and shaping of joy and life will improve and expand as we learn new ways to satisfy a diversity of new needs. And as we overcome the exclusive obsession with the genitals, we will find a new joy in an expansive erotic exchange that involves the entire body and goes beyond it to all the soft warm and wonder we feel from any thing and thought we share. Apart, we can still feel each other through a letter or call or a mellow memory played back slowly in our minds. Genital sex is not always necessary, and we can touch in our minds if we are really in tune and if we come to understand that feeling is not an exclusive function of the hands, but is primarily and more promisingly a function of the heart.

—Maulana Ron Karenga,[5] 1975

REFLECTION: Making love is extraordinary because it allows two people to share the incredible experience of oneness. The sensual sensations of lovemaking can engulf both lovers and transport them to a landscape of pleasure that can be both physical and spiritual. However, the blessing of sex is but one aspect of love. Love that centers on the genitals or on fleeting ardor is shallow at best. Physical desire must be balanced with tenderness, selflessness, and respect, both inside and outside of the bedroom. Real loving is about loving totally. Deep love moves beyond the five senses to encompass the heart, mind, and soul.

Deep love illuminates our entire being, touching both our body and soul.

LESSONS IN LOVE

Temperamentally, I'm much more concerned with the caring that lies beneath the antagonisms between black men and black women. There is a great deal of static that informs our relationships, above and beyond the political wedge that has been jammed between us by myth makers of the oppressor class. Whereas other writers, other women, other people, are more concerned with the hurt of it all, the hurt doesn't teach me anything and I'm concerned primarily with usable lessons.

—Toni Cade Bambara,[6] 1979

REFLECTION: If you've ever argued with a partner, you know that the quarrel can heat up to a point where the original issues no longer seem important. In the firestorm of the conflict, everything is reduced to winning or losing. No one listens—and nothing is ultimately resolved.

In the ongoing debate between Black men and women, too much emphasis has been placed on the emotional pain fueling the debate, rather than on the essential issues. From the face of the hurt caused by heated unresolved arguments, we develop grudges that eliminate any chance of resolution or reconciliation. We must commit to turning down the volume of the debate and initiate a true dialogue. Then and only then can love's most valuable lessons emerge.

When love becomes locked in hostility, it is far easier to embrace the pain than to learn the lesson. Today, I will resolve to listen and learn from conflict.

UNSELFISH LOVE

The separation between black man and black woman resets all national purpose and with that, all national spirit, broken down. A nation is a whole people. The black woman must be the one half and the black man must be the other half of our life sign, our eternal remanifestation. This has got to be easy to understand.

But as long as any thing separates the black man and the black woman from moving together, being together, being absolutely in tune, each doing what they supposed to, then the nation will never re-emerge. Our first step must be to reunderstand that we are simply different aspects of a single entity.

—Imamu Amiri Baraka,[7] 1970

REFLECTION: Take away love, and a family splinters. Take away love, and a people falters. Take away love, and life has little value. Both Black men and women have let outsiders—who do not have our best interests at heart—define our relationship to one another. Our scripts have been written elsewhere and quietly handed to us to act out.

We need a new kind of love that will promote healing. We need a love that will empower us to honor one another. Each time we lovingly work out our differences with one another, the spirit of reconciliation unites our whole community.

When we love ourselves, there is no limit to the love we can share. We need not confuse love with power or control. Real love is an act of faith and commitment.

I welcome the blessing of an unselfish, nation-building love.

SHOWING OUR LOVE

I love roses, but Medgar could never afford to buy me a florist's bouquet. So he did something better: Every year he made a ritual of giving me bare-root roses to plant in our front yard, and eventually, three dozen rosebushes were the envy of our neighbors. Once in a while, Medgar would gather a bouquet, or perhaps just one rose, and hand it to me as he came through the door. It became an unspoken verse of the love between us.

One night he came in rather late, and I knew, from the set of his shoulders, that he was unusually tired. But when he handed me a single red rose, I knew something else as well. The rose symbolized love. And the color red, for us at least, meant fire. In his own subtle way, Medgar had set the mood for the evening. He placed the rose in a beautiful cut-glass vase he'd given me one Christmas and placed it on the table. The children were asleep, and as usual, I warmed his dinner and set the table with our cherished silver candle holders. Medgar lit the candles. I sat with him while he ate and talked about his day. Afterward, we moved to the sofa and Medgar reclined, with his head in my lap. We stayed that way, in silence, for a while.

—Myrlie Evers,[8] 1986

REFLECTION: The love shared by Myrlie Evers and her late husband, Medgar Evers, was one that served as the foundation for much of the work accomplished by the heroic civil rights leader in the dangerous rural areas of Mississippi during the early 1960s. Theirs wasn't a showy love with a lot of theatrics and pomp. It was a mature love, a love that allowed them both the freedom to be themselves. Their relationship was based on mutual understanding and acceptance.

When one can be as open as Medgar was with his wife, it is not hard to understand how he was able to share his life with the world. His gift of roses was a delicate yet powerful display of a love that is unafraid to give totally of itself. True love is not selfish. Showing love in small, quiet ways means more than grand public displays of affection. It is the private, personal time together that helps us weather life's inevitable storms.

True love is the gift of giving freely and honestly of ourselves to one another.

Part 10

BLACK WOMEN AND BLACK MEN

WOMEN'S EQUALITY

I am above eighty years old; it is about time for me to be going. I have been forty years a slave and forty years free, and would be here forty years more to have equal rights for all. I suppose I am kept here because something remains for me to do; I suppose I am yet to help to break the chain. I have done a great deal of work; as much as a man, but did not get so much pay. I used to work in the field and bind grain, keeping up with the cradler; but men doing no more, got twice as much pay. . . . We do as much, we eat as much, we want as much. I suppose I am about the only colored woman that goes about to speak for the rights of the colored women. I want to keep the thing stirring, now that the ice is cracked. What we want is a little money. You men know that you get as much again as women, when you write, or for what you do. When we get our rights, we shall not have to come to you for money, for then we shall have money enough in our own pockets; and maybe you will ask us for money. But help us now until we get it. It is a good consolation to know that when we have got this battle once fought we shall not be coming to you any more.

—Sojourner Truth,[1] *1867*

REFLECTION: The cries of women for social and economic equality have long fallen on deaf ears. What do they want from us, some men ask? It's ironic that Sojourner Truth's words still ring true over 125 years later. One of the arguments lodged by opponents of affirmative action is that women now possess one-half of this country's wealth so there is no need for preferential treatment. Yet, statistics show that a substantial number of women are mired in poverty at the bottom of America's economic ladder.

Today, women are still battling gender bias to become firefighters, soldiers, judges, scientists, even sanitation workers. Some men still use the biological differences of women as a rationalization for their sexist views.

Women, especially African American women, are getting the job done every day! Maybe what some men fear is that once all obstacles to full economic and social access are lifted, women will no longer come to them to gather bits and pieces of their self-worth. No person should have to plead for what is theirs by birthright.

I refuse to let issues of race or gender cloud my judgment when assessing an individual's potential.

BLACK WOMEN

The Negro woman . . . is conscious that what is left of chivalry is not directed toward her. She realizes that the ideals of beauty, built up in the fine arts, have excluded her almost entirely. Instead, the grotesque Aunt Jemimas of the street-car advertisements, proclaim only an ability to serve, without grace of loveliness. Nor does the drama catch her finest spirit. She is most often used to provoke the mirthless laugh of ridicule; or to portray feminine viciousness or vulgarity not peculiar to Negroes. This is the shadow over her. To a race naturally sunny comes the twilight of self-doubt and a sense of personal inferiority. It cannot be denied that these are potent and detrimental influences, though not generally recognized because they are in the realm of the mental and spiritual.

—Elise Johnson McDougald,[2] 1925

REFLECTION: Today's images of African American women are still linked to the hurtful stereotypes of an earlier time—the noble mammy, the tragic mulatto, the available sexual object. These distortions have little to do with real life. The media myths portrayed in these twisted images are potent and numbing, binding us to old fears, old limitations, and old feelings of inferiority.

As Pearl Bailey used to say, "What do these people know about how I am, who I really am?" When we see images of African American women on television or in films, we must be vigilant in monitoring who controls these images. We must ask ourselves, are these images honest and accurate? Do they reflect African American women's true worth, complexity, and beauty?

Today, I will challenge any TV shows or movies that reinforce negative stereotypes of African American women. I will start a dialogue and take a stand.

LAYING DOWN THE BURDEN

From the days of slavery until now, we Black women have been given chores that sometimes were beyond our very strength . . . we can no longer afford to carry the burdens alone. Black women must be allowed to be women. I like in a woman something that is feminine, something that is gracious, something that is sweet.

If I may say so, the women of my race are tops. We're the cream.

—Amy Garvey, widow of Marcus Garvey,[3] 1973

REFLECTION: In recent years, African American women have been forced to carry more and more of the responsibility for the race. For generations, they have maintained our families' tenuous economic foothold, serving as our moral and spiritual compass while instilling a sense of pride and purpose in our children—often with little recognition or support from their partners or the society at large.

We should not be surprised if our women have grown weary under the weight of such tremendous expectations. Black women must be allowed to be more than saviors of the race—they must be allowed to be women!

I affirm African American women's right to lay their burdens down from time to time—and to revel in the experience of the sweetness of their femininity.

A GOOD WOMAN

Some women . . . have more influence than others. They're more persistent, persuasive, in a way of speaking. Give you more confidence. I see women as an inspiration, something to work for. It don't take a whole lot to satisfy a man. A woman gives a man something to go on, otherwise he's like a ship without a rudder with nobody to lead him on and give him inspiration.

—James Van Der Zee,[4] 1978

REFLECTION: When a man has lived alone for a while, he can come to truly value a good woman. Once the hormonal rush of youth is past, a man becomes more concerned with who his woman really is—the quality of her character and her generosity of soul. Her hair need not be long. She need not have a model's legs. She need not be a lady in the living room and a vixen in the bedroom.

Once a man understands the real benefits of a continuing relationship, he can appreciate a woman's true worth as a friend, helpmate, and lover. A wise man knows that being with a good woman is one of life's greatest rewards.

Who can measure the worth of a good woman? Today, I will truly acknowledge the love, support, and inspiration I receive from the woman in my life.

HEALING

Black brothers, please believe me, taking your hostility out on Black women is not the road to liberation. Neither is having her walk three paces behind you . . . the Black woman did not rob you of your manhood. Therefore, she cannot give it back to you. . . .

The Black woman is not the enemy, brother. She is your soul mate, the one who has given her strength to the struggle down through the years. Black women and Black men must march hand-in-hand down the road to liberation. This is the only path to freedom.

—John O. Killens,[5] *1973*

REFLECTION: Many Black men are bewildered by the battle of the sexes. They are baffled by male-bashing and do not know how to act with women anymore. Many believed that showing their sensitive side and crying in front of women might do the trick; they were dismissed as wimps. Others considered a return to the caveman macho approach, saying the sisters need to know who's the boss. Some decided to use women solely as sex objects. Others have hidden out in their jobs.

As John O. Killens aptly states, Black women are not the enemy. Black men must stop oppressing Black women as a way of bolstering their embattled manhood. It's time to figure out what is important to us as a people. We need to listen to one another. We need to start a healing dialogue before the damage becomes irreparable.

Black women are not the cause of Black men's failings. The healing will begin once we are able to join hands.

THE REAL BLACK MAN

We must stand up now or forever remain a fallen race. For we must recognize that we are now stumbling, but at the same time—and almost in contradiction—that "to stumble is not to fall but to go forward faster." One can stumble and fall, but by definition one does not fall when he merely stumbles; and neither does a people resting on the shoulders of the male, the black male.

There are only two basic kinds of black men—the broken who fall and the true black man who may have stumbled in the past but will rise again.

We as black men are breaking loose, with each passing day, from the shackles that bind us, both physical and mental, and becoming once again the real black man in the full tradition of our pre-European forebears.

We are rising and we will win. Victory is ours to seize, if we will but stand and seize it.

Will the real black man please stand up?

—Nathan Hare,[6] 1971

REFLECTION: Black women often ask: Where are the real Black men? They point to the sobering statistics about how many of our men are in prison, on drugs, unemployed—or dead.

What the data does not say is that there are still a great many good, stable, responsible Black men out there. Men who go to work every day, support their families, spend time with their children, and take a stand for the survival of our people.

Throughout our history, African American men have proven themselves again and again as fathers, warriors, and leaders. That quality has not died in our race. But good Black men have been too quiet for too long. Now is the time for our strong men to stand up and let their presence be felt in our communities.

I support the efforts of good Black men who come forward and do their part.

BLACK MEN

Black men must be believers in Black people (men, women, and children) twenty-four hours a day and develop a lifestyle that clearly states we are not for sale.

There is loneliness in our lives. Even in the roar of the crowd we find that our connection to that which is natural and real is often the superficial interpretations of others. Our ability to feel lessens as our world becomes more concrete and individualized. It is not enough that our food is plastic, our water undrinkable, that we are driven from our families because we can't support them; but when human and spiritual bonds that have for so long sustained us in unbearable hours fade away—it is time for urgent reassessment. We are a social people and the Black family has been the foundation of our strength. This foundation is weakened when the men are confused about their role, rather, their mission in life.

—Haki R. Madhubuti,[7] 1979

REFLECTION: A lot of African American men are infected with a near-lethal dose of self-pity. They bemoan the avalanche of criticism being heaped on them from every quarter. Some say: "Why should I get all worked up about what people are saying about me? They don't care about me no way." Many men feel that there's no one praising their hard work and commitment. Not all Black men are bailing out of their obligations. Not all are seeking a blissful escape in drink and drugs.

Nevertheless, the Black family has been rocked to its foundation by the highly visible number of men who do not know what to do to regain their rightful position in their families and in their communities. They are lost. No people can construct the security of its community upon the insecurity of its men. Much of the collective damage could be reversed if black men were courageous enough to acknowledge past mistakes and return to help shoulder the responsibility of the family. Every transgression would not be forgotten, but a great deal would be forgiven.

Black men can best serve their families and their communities by expecting and demanding more of themselves.

SEX OBJECTS

I resent it that ill and fearful minds attribute to the manhood and humanness of the dark-skinned male an unfounded characteristic so loaded with emotional content. It has aroused unnatural fear and curiosity among many white women; it has aroused fear and jealousy among white men. It is a matter of indifference to Negro women, whose main concern is having a family life with the male. An erroneous and evil sex emphasis has handicapped the decent human relations to which society ought to commit itself.

—Dorothy Dandridge,[8] 1970

REFLECTION: One of the most powerful ills of bigotry in the history of African Americans has been white society's demonization of the Black male. The Black man was seen as a savage beast, a lusty animal of minimal intelligence and uncontrollable passions, a dreaded creature capable of unspeakable acts. These images were used to justify the rash of lynchings that followed Reconstruction and extended into the first sixty years of this century.

The fears upon which these brutal crimes were based still exist. Some say these fears propelled the national obsessions with the Mike Tyson and O. J. Simpson trials. In many ways, Black men flirt with the image of sexual superiority as one of the few ways of goading white males, but the consequences of using such a stereotype have been disastrous in the past and continue to be so in the present. Nothing is more tragic than a man or woman reduced to a distorted stereotype that violates their humanity. No Black man or woman should allow members of our race to be dehumanized in this manner.

I will challenge all attempts to negate my humanity with negative sexual stereotypes.

RESPONSIBLE MANHOOD

For the black man in this country, it is not so much a matter of acquiring manhood as it is a struggle to feel it his own. Whereas the white man regards his manhood as an ordained right, the black man is engaged in a never-ending battle for its possession. For the black man, attaining any portion of manhood is an active process. He must penetrate barriers and overcome opposition in order to assume a masculine posture. For the inner psychological obstacles to manhood are never so formidable as the impediments woven into American society. . . .

Throughout his life, at each critical point of development the black boy is told to hold back, to constrict, to subvert and camouflage his normal masculinity. Male assertiveness becomes a forbidden fruit, and if it is attained, it must be savored privately.

—William H. Grier, M.D., and Price M. Cobbs, M.D.,[9] 1968

REFLECTION: What it means to be a man is a controversial issue in the contemporary African American community. Young Black men often enter manhood confused and angry. They have few role models. There is no manual on Black manhood. Many of our young men were raised in female-headed single households where survival often took precedence over socialization. They express their manliness in gold chains, designer jackets, and high-powered guns. Not being "dissed" has become the yardstick for masculinity. Daily newspapers carry the latest reports on their uniquely American tragedy, their young lives lost to murder or drugs and destroyed by adolescent rage.

There is much more to being a Black man in white America. It demands effort, tenacity, discipline, and responsible actions to meet the challenges of daily life.

Today, I will demonstrate my manhood in acts of personal excellence and achievement.

Part 11

A Living
God

GOD CREATED US EQUAL

God saw fit to vary everything in nature. There are no two men alike—no two voices alike—no two trees alike. God has weaved and tissued variety and versatility throughout the boundless space of His creation. Because God saw fit to make some red, and some white, and some black, and some brown, are we to sit here in judgment upon what God has seen fit to do? As well might one play with the thunderbolts of heaven as with that creature that bears God's image—God's photograph.

—Henry McNeal Turner,[1] 1868

REFLECTION: During the post–Civil War era of Reconstruction in America, a scientific and theological argument raged over whether the Negro was closer to the beasts of the field than to the other races of humans on earth. Henry McNeal Turner's blistering defense of the humanity of his people still rings true today as that ancient debate continues, with more pseudo-scientific studies denigrating the humanity and intelligence of the African American.

Noted intellectual St. Clair Drake often remarked that many of our problems as a race stem from our failed belief in our own humanity. This lack of self-worth is very evident today. It remains a powerful tool in our own oppression, and because it is so insidious, it's often difficult to overcome. To live as human beings, we must affirm our fundamental equality. We are all equal, regardless of color, race, or gender. God created us all, created us equal.

I refuse to question my humanity or my equality. My existence bears the indelible stamp of the Almighty.

OUR STRONGEST ALLY

Ah America, you should never have brought the black man to your shores and let him taste for a moment the sweet atmosphere of the liberty that you enjoyed. For once tasted, it becomes so palatable that nothing can satisfy the appetite but to savor of it fully. You should never have sent your doctrine of Christianity to the slave cabins and cotton fields if you did not fully mean or understand your own creed. Your ideas fell on an imaginative and passionate race which eagerly grasped your words and gave them a new sound. Your Christ became, first a song hummed by an old field hand, and later a way of thinking—a way of life. While you timidly sang of your Christianity, the Negro shouted his and found in it so much sweetness that it had to be shared with another—and still another.

—Annetta G. Jefferson,[2] 1961

REFLECTION: In the beginning, the slave-traders used Christianity to justify the practice of slavery. The slave-owner quoted from the Bible, citing the curse of Ham to defend the enslaving of his Black brethren, while continuing to declare that he loved his neighbor as himself. This twisted interpretation of God's teaching was also used to subdue Blacks into thinking that the Creator had deserted them.

Someone once said that "no one could ever say Christianity has failed because it has never been tried." But African Americans tried it somewhere along the way; Blacks learned to read and interpret the Bible for themselves. In the torment of our bondage, we took the faith of our captors, culled out the best of its tenets, and used it to sustain us on the road to our salvation and triumph.

Through eyes cleared of the veil of deceit, the theology of oppression became transformed into a theology of liberation and salvation. We molded this new faith to strengthen our resolve during rough times, and to serve as a guide for spiritual gratitude during times of celebration.

My life has purpose, my faith is strong. My love of God, life, and freedom increases every day.

HEAVEN ON EARTH

I believe that hell and heaven that are depicted in the Bible are descriptive of a condition of the human spirit. Hell is to be cut off from God and His Presence. Heaven is to be with God. . . . I believe in sowing and reaping, and reward and punishment in life. The extent to which the moral law operates beyond death is not ours to know. Because I believe that death is something that is experienced in life and not to life. I do not think that the matter of death as such has any bearing on the moral law whatsoever.

—Dr. Howard Thurman,[3] *1961*

REFLECTION: The spiritual notions of heaven and hell are hard to comprehend. Remember Malcolm X's call for us to reclaim heaven for ourselves right here on earth. He insisted that we cannot afford to wait to enjoy its milk and honey. One of our greatest problems is that we have been too quick to postpone everything. Some of us postpone living for fear that we will miss heaven. Others postpone taking steps to change the directions of our lives, thinking that there will always be a tomorrow.

As Dr. Thurman said, life is about sowing and reaping, rewards and punishments, cause and effect. Death will someday come to us all. For this reason, we must seek our taste of heaven now. We have no idea what awaits on the "other side," so we must leap into the business of life with both feet.

Everything we do now has consequences. Even doing nothing produces results. Don't hold anything back. The Great Beyond can wait. Live now—as though your life depends on it!

I will not postpone life. I will live fully in the now!

THE FAITHFUL

I have the soundest of reasons for being proud of my people. We Negroes have always had such a tough time that our very survival in this white world with the dice always loaded against us is the greatest possible testimonial to our strength, our courage, and our immunity to adversity.

We are close to this earth and to God. Shut up in ghettos, sneered at, beaten, enslaved, we always have answered our oppressors with brave singing, dancing, and laughing. Our greatest eloquence, the pith of the joy and sorrow in our unbreakable hearts, comes when we lift up our faces and talk to God, person to person. Ours is the truest dignity of man, the dignity of the undefeated.

—Ethel Waters,[4] 1951

REFLECTION: With each passing day, we realize more and more that it is the many blessings of the Creator that have allowed our people to survive and thrive in the toughest of times.

The elders often talk about picking cotton under a sizzling hot July sun, dragging the long bag full of white bolls with swollen aching hands. They say they didn't know how they would make it to the next day. Sometimes they were so tired that they fell asleep before they could eat dinner. Sometimes they ached so bad they couldn't straighten out the next morning. But still their feet kept moving over the red clay from dawn to dusk. Not one of them would deny that their strength, their endurance, came from their unshakable faith and their ceaseless prayers. That was how they crossed over the River Jordan.

I know that with faith and prayer I will never be defeated.

GOD HELPS THOSE . . .

I told you how I say the Lord's Prayer every night before I go to bed. And from time to time I've been known to pray for other reasons. But that's only after I've done all I could on my own. Far as I'm concerned, it's stupid to go to God every time you prick your finger or stub your toe. You don't want to use up your favors or exhaust God's patience.

I say: As long as I can stand it, God, I'll keep on keeping on. I say: When I can do a little bit more on my own, Lord, I'll do it. I say: If I have strength left in me, then I'll use it.

Mama said, and I still believe her, that God helps those who help themselves. Now that's the truth.

—Ray Charles,[5] 1978

REFLECTION: How many of us go to God with a laundry list? God, give me a big raise. God, give me a new car. God, send me a man or a woman with money. We're like children asking our parents for the most popular Christmas toys. Disappointment and doubt are sure to set in when such requests go unanswered.

But there's another way to go to God. The beginning of an answered prayer is the desire to work in partnership with the Creator. We're working with the Creator when we ask for blessings tied to whole-life transformations, when we call on God for grace and support, when we ask for guidance that helps us live fuller, more loving lives. The Creator hears us best when our request is heartfelt and our need is great.

I will make every prayer count.

THE BLACK CHURCH

Despite our new worldliness, despite our rhythms, our colorful speech, and our songs, we keep our churches alive. In fact, we have built more of them than ever here on the city pavements, for it is only when we are within the walls of our churches that we are wholly ourselves, that we keep alive a sense of our personalities in relation to the total world in which we live, that we maintain a quiet and constant communion with all that is deepest in us. Our going to church on a Sunday is like placing one's ear to another's chest to hear the unquenchable murmur of the human heart. In our collective outpourings of song and prayer, the fluid emotions of others make us feel the strength in ourselves.

—Richard Wright,[6] 1941

REFLECTION: There is a power in the union of souls. The Black church has long been our refuge, our strength, and our inspiration. It was here that we plotted our freedom. It was here that we learned the potency of language and song. It was here that we bred our leaders. It was here that the Creator took human form and walked among us. It was here that we were not afraid. It was here that we could rejoice without fear of any reproach or reprisal. It was here that we spoke with one voice.

I will come together with others to worship in the fellowship of the Black Church to add might to my soul.

AN ACTIVE FAITH

Religion has been a civilizing influence in almost every society in which it has been featured, and I think if we need anything at all at the moment, we need a return toward the civilizing and humanizing aspects of society to help save us from what seems to be an overcentralization of society and a loss of many of the cardinal values which have, in the past, helped to hold society together and to make it a safe and reasonable place in which to live. . . .

. . . There have certainly been periods in our history in which the opportunity for any kind of aggressive expression of Black militancy would have been completely suicidal. In these instances the Black church filled the void in a way that made survival possible and made life livable, so to speak. Now there is no longer this necessity. The Black church can now express itself in any way it chooses. We do not have to be an ultra-mundane society; we do not have to look for our rewards on the other side of Jordan. We can look for them now, and we can struggle for them now, and the Black church could well be the instrument by which this struggle might be launched.

—Dr. C. Eric Lincoln,[7] *1976*

REFLECTION: A movement is under way in certain segments of the Black Church to return to its early activist origins. Some people are using the teachings of the Gospel to energize the faithful and get them out on the streets to where the Holy Word has been absent lately.

The work is being done on a national scale. In almost every city, churches are instituting youth intervention programs, fatherhood counseling seminars, and other outreach efforts to better serve their communities. This spiritual revolution in the house of the Creator can energize all of us with a transformed vision of the role of the Divine in our quest for freedom and equality.

I will support the activist legacy of the Black Church by donating my time and services at my house of worship.

FAITH

In the midst of outer dangers I have felt an inner calm and known resources of strength that only God could give. In many instances I have felt the power of God transforming the fatigue of despair into the buoyancy of hope. I am convinced that the universe is under the control of a loving purpose and that in the struggle for righteousness, man has cosmic companionship. Behind the harsh appearances of the world there is a benign power. To say God is personal is not to make him an object among other objects or to attribute to him the finiteness and limitations of human personality; it is to take what is finest and noblest in our consciousness and affirm its perfect existence in him. It is certainly true that human personality is limited, but personality as such involves no necessary limitations. It simply means self-consciousness and self-direction. So in the truest sense of the word, God is a living God. In him there is feeling and will, responsive to the deepest yearnings of the human heart: this God both evokes and answers prayers.

—Martin Luther King, Jr.,[8] *1958*

REFLECTION: A woman was driving in a blinding rainstorm, with three of her girlfriends, along a steep, winding road bounded on one side by a deep ravine. The car seemed to be holding its own against the deluge. Suddenly, it felt as though the ground had been yanked out from under them and the vehicle became airborne. It cleared the railing and sailed out into the rain and fog over the tops of the trees. As the car plunged toward the ravine, the woman sat back in her seat, her fingers gripping the steering wheel. Despite the horrifying screams of her friends in the background, she felt intensely calm and serene. She whispered a short prayer for God's grace just before the car struck the ground, and then a white flash enveloped her consciousness. Everyone survived despite the tremendous crash. As the woman was loaded into an ambulance, there were tears in her eyes and the only words on her bruised lips were: "Thank you, God. You heard me."

Faith in the Creator is rewarded with miracle after miracle, some seen, others unseen.

My faith in the Creator is rewarded many times throughout the day. My life is filled with miracles.

PARTNERSHIP WITH GOD

In the midst of the most stifling circumstances, this belief in God has given the Negro masses emotional poise and balance; it has enabled them to cling on to life though poor, miserable, and dying, looking to God and expecting Him, through miraculous and spectacular means, to deliver them from their plight. The idea has made Negroes feel good; it has made life endurable for them; and it has caused them to go to church on Sunday and shout and sing and pray. It has sent them back to their unbearable situations on Monday strengthened to carry on another week, consoled by the fact that "troubles don't last always."

—Benjamin E. Mays,[9] 1938

REFLECTION: It is rare for our journey with the Creator to be an entirely smooth one. Like all relationships, there will be troubling disputes and long silences along the way. There are many occasions when God's miraculous support comes as a powerful blessing. At other times, when troubles are piling up and relief is nowhere in sight, it feels nonexistent. There are moments when we have to go forward under our own steam, when we must use our God-given free will, knowing that the hand of the Divine moves in our lives even in the most oppressive of circumstances. That's how we learn to co-create our lives in partnership with God.

I'm grateful for the chance to show myself—and God—what I can do.

GOD OF LOVE

I believe that God is a merciful God and therefore He has provided the means of redemption to expiate our sins. But He would not require eternal payment. Heaven is a state of serenity. Doing good provides the immediate reward of satisfaction and also the later enjoyment of reflection. The concept of hell in its fiery form is valuable because fear of punishment is a restraining influence which has kept many people out of hell. However, the purpose of the ministry is to lift up the hope of heaven and win people to righteous living rather than frighten them. To make this choice is to achieve paradise here and hereafter.

—Dr. Archibald J. Carey, Jr.,[10] 1961

REFLECTION: The God of my youth was a frightening, vengeful God who rarely showed mercy. He was to be feared even more than the eternal flames and torments of Hell. He never seemed to show much sympathy or compassion for the faithless, the fallen, or the lost.

The God of my maturity is just the opposite. Over the years, I began to discover for myself that the Creator is not a God of wrath or punishment. The Creator is a kind, loving, and caring God, a firm but compassionate teacher.

Sometimes, like children, we grow obsessed with the darker, vengeful side of the Omnipotent. We see God as a merciless power who intervenes in our lives on whim or caprice—often not in our favor. Now is the time for us to change our perspective. Now is the time for us to see God as the source of divine blessings and mercy, not of retribution and retaliation.

Today, I will view my Creator in a new light. I will welcome this loving Divine Force into my life.

GOD LOVES FUN

I've had my fun. He made this earth for man to have some fun in. Enjoy. The one thing He don't want you to do is mistreat a man or woman. He love people. He want you to love one another as he love you. I love all people. I love everything God made. I pray to feel that way. I want to be the best loving man in the world.

God will always be the heavenly father and the ruler, as long as you see that sun rise and that moon at night. As long as the tree have leaves, He will be king. 'Cause he is life.

—Roosevelt Sykes,[11] 1975

REFLECTION: Despite the Western image of the Creator as a poker-faced old man with a long white beard, God's sense of fun shows up in His creations. Think of the platypus, the kangaroo, the giraffe, the alligator, and the elephant.

But you know God has a great sense of humor when you take a look at the way people behave. Walk through any city or neighborhood in America and quietly observe the men and women in action. Human beings are hilarious. You get a whole different perspective on what we're doing here on Earth when you realize that people are God's way of having fun.

When we laugh and have fun, we know God is laughing right along with us. Today, I will enjoy life—for God's sake as well as my own.

Part 12

RACE AND RACISM

THE TRUTH

Sir, I freely and cheerfully acknowledge, that I am of the African race, and in that color which is natural to them of the deepest dye; and it is under a sense of the most profound gratitude to the Supreme Ruler of the Universe, that I now confess to you, that I am not under that state of tyrannical thraldom, and inhuman captivity, to which too many of my brethren are doomed, but that I have abundantly tasted of the fruition of those blessings, which proceed from that free and unequalled liberty with which you are favored; and which, I hope, you will willingly allow you have mercifully received, from the immediate hand of that Being, from whom proceedeth every good and perfect Gift. . . .

I suppose that your knowledge of the situation of my brethren, is too extensive to need a recital here; neither shall I presume to prescribe methods by which they may be received, otherwise than by recommending to you and all others, to wean yourselves from those narrow prejudices which you have imbibed with respect to them, and as Job proposed to his friends, 'put your soul in their souls' stead'; thus shall your hearts be enlarged with kindness and benevolence towards them; and thus shall you need neither the direction of myself or others, in what manner to proceed herein.

—Benjamin Banneker,[1] 1791

REFLECTION: Benjamin Banneker, mathematician and astronomer, was a man who loved to share information, to illuminate the lives of others. In 1791, he began to publish a series of almanacs that became very popular in the states of Pennsylvania, Delaware, Maryland, and Virginia. They were a household staple in early America. Banneker, who would serve prominently on a commission to design the nation's capitol, also wrote several letters to Thomas Jefferson, then secretary of state, on the question of race and slavery.

Jefferson, a true politician, replied: "Nobody wishes more than I do to see such proofs as you exhibit that nature has given to our black brethren talents equal to those of the other colors of men." The examples set by such intelligent Blacks as Banneker made the myths of race and slavery difficult for Jefferson and others to justify. Jefferson knew the myths were lies just as those in power today know that the myths of latter-day racism are false. Basic human truths cannot be denied.

I seek to illuminate every situation with truth.

BREAKING THE CHAINS

For the moment the dreams of my youth and the hopes of my manhood were completely fulfilled. The bonds that had held me to "old master" were broken. No man now had a right to call me his slave or assert mastery over me. . . . A new world had opened upon me. If life is more than breath, and the "quick round of blood," I lived more in one day than in a year of my slave life. It was a time of joyous excitement which words can but tamely describe. . . . A contest had in fact been going on in my mind for a long time, between the clear consciousness of right and the plausible makeshifts of theology and superstition. The one held me an abject slave—a prisoner for life, punished for some transgressions in which I had no lot or part; the other counseled me to manly endeavor to secure my freedom. This contest was now ended, my chains were broken, and the victory brought me unspeakable joy.

—Frederick Douglass,[2] 1892

REFLECTION: Even though we're no longer slaves, many of us are not free. We're still held in psychic bondage by a society that questions our innate abilities, exploits our talents, and even threatens our right to be. The damage caused by the invisible chains of racism might even be more insidious than the visible chains of slavery because, after all, we're supposed to be free!

Frederick Douglass was elated when his physical chains were broken and his spiritual liberation could begin. From burning crosses to *The Bell Curve*, we live in a society that offers racism as daily bread. We must continue to ask ourselves what psychological freedom would feel like. We must ask how can we liberate our spirits in the face of racism's daily assault.

What would it feel like to be able to spend twenty-four hours without bearing the burden of race? Today, there is nowhere to run. We must free ourselves from the inside out.

Today, we must work together to find new ways to be free men and women. We must accept nothing less than psychological liberation.

LEARNING FROM THE PAST

Perhaps those of us who can admit we are imprisoned by the history of racial subordination in America can accept—as slaves had no choice but to accept—our fate. Not that we legitimate the racism of the oppressor. On the contrary, we can only delegitimate it if we can accurately pinpoint it. And racism lies at the center, not the periphery; in the permanent, not in the fleeting; in the real lives of black and white people, not in the sentimental caverns of the mind.

Armed with this knowledge, and with the enlightened, humility-based commitment that it engenders, we can accept the dilemmas of committed confrontation with evils we cannot end. We can go forth to serve, knowing that our failure to act will not change conditions and may very well worsen them. We can listen carefully to those who have been subordinated. In listening, we must not do them the injustice of failing to recognize that somehow they survived as complete, defiant, though horribly scarred beings. We must learn from their example, learn from those whom we would teach.

If we are to extract solutions from the lessons of the slaves' survival, and our own, we must first face squarely the unbearable landscape and climate of that survival.

—Derrick Bell,[3] 1992

REFLECTION: Author Derrick Bell has been very precise in detailing what surviving slavery did to the African American psyche. In exacting terms, he explains its huge toll on us and its influence in molding how we view every significant area of our lives.

As a people, we learned good and bad things from the experience. However, many of the plantation survival skills we acquired during that long, agonizing travail can be discarded because we no longer have use for them. We must thoroughly examine our psychological history as well as our cultural history to determine what we shall keep and what must be tossed aside. And it's a good time to do the same thing in our personal lives. We should look within our hearts and souls, and cull out those things that are no longer useful to us. We can no longer afford to hold on to parts of ourselves that do not benefit us. It's time to clean house.

I will master the lessons of my ancestors' example and retain only those survival skills that benefit me.

ENDING RACISM

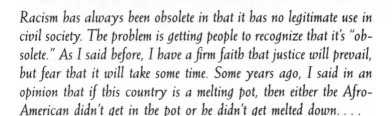

Racism has always been obsolete in that it has no legitimate use in civil society. The problem is getting people to recognize that it's "obsolete." As I said before, I have a firm faith that justice will prevail, but fear that it will take some time. Some years ago, I said in an opinion that if this country is a melting pot, then either the Afro-American didn't get in the pot or he didn't get melted down. . . .

I would repeat the story of my good friend William Coleman. He says he looks forward to the day when an Afro-American gets on the commuter train in Connecticut early one morning to go to his job on Wall Street. He has a derby hat, Brooks Brothers suit, New York Times, Wall Street Journal under his arm, and a beat-up but not too beat-up briefcase, and he sits down and reads the paper. And as the train makes stops people get on, get on, get on and it gets crowded. And a white woman gets on down the line and there is only one seat vacant in the whole car, and that's beside the Afro-American. And she looks all around and she can't find any other seat so she has to sit down beside him, and as she sits down, she just can't stand it any longer and she yells "niggers, niggers, niggers!" And the Afro-American jumps up and says, "Where? Where? Where?" Now that's what I'm waiting for, that day.

— *Justice Thurgood Marshall,*[4] *1990*

REFLECTION: Americans have a hard time acknowledging the existence of racism and racists. Racism, as they see it today, only rears its ugly head on rare occasions and not with the same force or ferocity of years gone by.

In the minds of these people, our society is nearly color-blind, with tolerance and equal opportunity available to all. They see racism and discrimination as crutches used by African Americans and other people of color to avoid the hard work of achievement and accomplishment. Or, as one white man recently told me: "Gee, Bob, you can't blame whites living today for slavery and things done to you guys before we were born."

Anyone who says racism no longer exists is in denial. What was the Rodney King incident? What happened in Howard Beach and Bensonhurst? The list is a lengthy one that never seems to stop growing. Racism is directed not only toward blacks but toward all people of color here in the daily commerce of life. We are all NIGGERS in the eyes of the racist. Like Justice Marshall, we all long for the day when someone cries "nigger," and there will be no "nigger" to be found.

I work for the day when racism will be meaningless and obsolete.

BIGOTRY

I felt like saying: "How big does a person have to grow, down in this part of the country, before he's going to stand up and say—Let us stop treating other men and women and children with such cruelty just 'cause they are born colored!"

From the days of slavery, black men have worked inside white people's homes as pantry men, butlers, and chauffeurs, helping bring up little boys and girls, and taking pride in being a trusted part of the family. Up north today many families rely on black maids and baby sitters. So if they trust their most cherished possession—their child—to us, tell me, how can they have such hate and fear of us?

—Mahalia Jackson,[5] 1955

REFLECTION: It's early afternoon on a summer day. One section of the park is filled with Black women supervising the activities of young white children. The youngsters run and jump and chase one another within the sight of their guardians. One Black woman, holding a small white boy crying after a fall, says to another caretaker: "The family I'm with now is so much better than the last one. I put all my time into that little monster, raising him up from a wee baby, and he comes up and calls me nigger one day. It hurt me to my heart."

The other woman watched her young charge out of the corner of her eye and asked: "What did the parents do when you told them?"

The first woman clutched the little boy closer to her bosom, answering: "The mother said he must have picked the word up from his playmates. Said I shouldn't worry about it, no big thing. I quit the next day. It hurt so much because I spent more time with that boy growing up than my own."

Prejudice confounds all logical thought. I will not waste my energy trying to understand or rationalize bigotry.

NEUTRALIZING RACISM

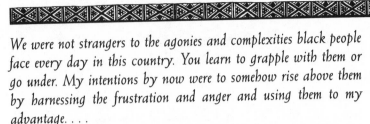

We were not strangers to the agonies and complexities black people face every day in this country. You learn to grapple with them or go under. My intentions by now were to somehow rise above them by harnessing the frustration and anger and using them to my advantage. . . .

. . . The present surge of bigotry I see in this nation warns us that the enemy is regrouping. But then so are young black rebels. Racism seems ageless—like the passion of those who war against it.

—*Gordon Parks,*[6] *1990*

REFLECTION: Nothing can ruin a good day like a racist determined to show you that Jim Crow is not dead. If you're having a bout of low self-esteem or an acute case of self-consciousness, the experience can penetrate right down to your soul. The bigot can be a cashier who ignores you and waits on the white person in line behind you first. The bigot can be a policeman harassing you for a marginal traffic infraction or the woman at the real estate office who says the property is sold when your Black face comes into view. Experiences like these happen to Black people every day.

No one suggests that you respond to everyday racism by smiling sheepishly, nodding your head, and shuffling away. But neither should you succumb to rage or bitterness. It is your right as an American citizen to protest discourteous behavior in a firm but reasonable way. You should make your point and move on. Never let the ignorance of others make you feel less than human. By channeling the anger caused by racism into positive action, we soar above the trap of hatred.

Today, I will react responsibly to racism. I will take action and move on.

A DIVIDED SOCIETY

We misunderstand racism completely if we do not understand that racism is a mask for a much deeper problem involving not the victims of racism but the perpetrators. We must come to see that racism in America is the poor man's way out and the powerful man's way in: a way in for the powerful who derive enormous profits from the divisions in our society. . . .

. . . Growing up in a culture permeated with prejudice, imbibing it, so to speak, with their milk, millions of white Americans find that Negroes are useful screens to hide themselves from themselves. Repeated studies have shown that Negro hate is, in part, a socially-sanctioned outlet for personal and social anxieties and frustrations. From this standpoint, racism is a flight from the self, a flight from freedom, a flight from the intolerable burdens of being a man in a menacing world.

—Lerone Bennett,[7] *1965*

REFLECTION: No one in America can be truly free as long as racism remains a powerful tool for political, social, and cultural control. Who needs the propaganda of the Ku Klux Klan when we have the powerful image manipulation of the media? They stake out a piece of the public consciousness for advertising dollars and then develop a strategy to exploit racial clichés.

We witness racism today when an unknown Black man is conjured up as a fearsome devil invoked to hide crimes committed by whites. Susan Smith claimed a Black man kidnapped her children, when she had actually drowned them to keep her lover. And Willie Horton's demonized image was used to bolster the conservative ticket in the Bush presidential campaign. Blame a Black man and get away with murder!

All of these incidents carry the stench of racism. And none of us—Black or white—can ever be free as long as racism remains a driving force in America. It not only prevents us from seeing others clearly, it also keeps us from seeing ourselves.

Battling racism in all its forms is the price of freedom.

SPEAKING UP

We need to step up the fight against the forces denying complete free-dom to all people and spend much less time gloating, as it were, over the gains we have made in the past.

I feel this way so strongly that I know I may have rubbed others the wrong way by things I've said; and many have called me a controversial figure. Certainly it is a fact that I have "sounded off" on issues when I might well have kept silent and avoided the labels "aggressive," "impatient," and "troublemaker." Epithets have not changed my convictions, however. When I see examples of injustice, persecution, intolerance, or other violations of basic ethics, I have to speak out. And I am convinced that it is only by speaking out and by acting through every legitimate means available that we can bring about desired change.

—Jackie Robinson,[8] *1969*

REFLECTION: Sometimes one person taking a stand against injustice can turn the tide of history. Rosa Parks did it by refusing to give up her bus seat after a tiring day in Montgomery, Alabama, and her action gave rise to the Civil Rights Movement. Many issues today have no one to champion them: affirmative action; redlining; welfare reform; voting rights; first-class education for our children. Not every battle seems so monumental or historic when it's being fought. But when we look the other way in the face of injustice, we become co-conspirators in our own oppression. We must get involved. We must speak up. Silence is neither golden nor wise.

Today, I will speak out and take a stand in the fight against racism, injustice, and oppression.

Part 13

FREEDOM

STRIKING THE BLOW

Who would be free themselves must strike the blow. We do not believe, as we are often told, that the Negro is the ugly child of the National family, and the more he is kept out of sight the better it will be for him. You know that liberty given is never so precious as liberty sought for and fought for. The man outraged is the man to make the outcry. Depend upon it, men will not care much for a people who do not care for themselves.

—Frederick Douglass,[1] 1882

REFLECTION: African Americans decided shortly after our arrival on American shores that we were going to live. Our extraordinary will took possession of our souls and we daily rekindled our vow to survive in those early, grim days. Throughout the years, we have renegotiated our contract with freedom again and again, demanding more each time than the limited privileges granted earlier.

Striving for freedom meant taking the blows of injustice, occasionally staggering from the pain, but never ceasing to press forward. Some of us gave up back then. Some of us give up now. But the majority of African Americans are survivors. We tire of the struggle sometimes and think of surrender—but we don't. We're committed to attaining the next phase of our freedom. We're committed to our children. We're committed to success and prosperity. We are committed to the survival of our race.

Today, I will strike a blow for freedom in my thoughts and actions. I will not only survive, I will thrive.

FREEDOM

If white men are afraid of fear, Negroes are ofttimes afraid of freedom. Freedom involves the confrontation of the unknown, the untried. It is a call to leave the familiarity of the usual for the possibilities inherent in what is unusual. . . . Three hundred years of bondage and quasi-bondage have taken an understandable toll in constructive energy and self-respect. . . .

That men shall be free is the irrepressible dictate of the moral law. Men must be free whether they will or not, for without freedom there is no responsibility, and responsibility is man's charter for participation in the historical process.

—Dr. C. Eric Lincoln,[2] 1960

REFLECTION: When we are small, we yearn for freedom and autonomy without understanding its awesome responsibility. Black people understand the idea of freedom in a very real sense, yet we hesitate to own its power, and to use this power to forge ahead. Freedom is a dangerous idea for so many of us because it implies seizing the responsibility for our future. We must not fear freedom. We must allow its light to penetrate into every cell of our being.

Even though we're still constrained by racism and discrimination, we are freer today than ever, freer to respond to life's challenges and succeed, but also freer to do nothing and stagnate. The door to a fuller, richer, more productive life lies open, but often we pause, fearful of the choices that await us.

Many of us live our lives by committee, asking others to make our decisions for us. When we do this, we are still slaves. Freedom means that we take complete responsibility for our choices and our lives. Knowing that the life we are living is truly our own creation is one of life's greatest joys. That is real freedom.

Today, nothing and no one will prevent me from exercising total freedom in my life.

TRUTH

Truth cannot be separated from the people's struggle and the hopes and dreams that arise from that struggle. Truth is that transcendent reality, disclosed in the people's historical struggle for liberation, which enables them to know that their fight for freedom is not futile. The affirmation of truth means that the freedom hoped for will be realized. Indeed, the freedom hoped for is already partly realized in our present history, because the realization of hope is the very ground of our present struggle. We do not struggle in despair but in hope, not from doubt but from faith, not out of hate but out of love for ourselves and for humanity.

—James Cone,[3] 1976

REFLECTION: In American politics, there is something called a "half-truth." But this, in itself, is a lie. Either something is the truth or it isn't. Historically, African Americans have been the victims of a deluge of half-truths, all designed to soothe, quiet, and pacify them in their struggle for full human rights.

However, truth is a quality beyond facts, beyond words, beyond time. Truth is the enemy of any disguised lie. Truth has no limits. And the truth of our situation is that Black Americans are still denied the same rights and privileges as white Americans. The truth is that our struggle continues.

The truth will set all of us free.

NATURE'S PLAN

*I go for freedom, but freedom without organization is chaos. . . .
You've got to take memory from the universe. Man will never organize anything as well as nature can. It's perpetual, but so many
things are happening that you always discover something else in
nature. It's organized and you find out it's doing the same thing all
the time.*

—Dizzy Gillespie,[4] 1977

REFLECTION: Sometimes our difficulties are the result of letting our lives get so free-form that there's no order at all. We go from one crisis to the next because we have a plan for the future.

Back in our grandparents' time, there was the traditional Sunday dinner where the family discussed where they were and what lay ahead. Understanding that they were born poor, they were determined not to die that way. They understood that upward mobility meant you had to have values, education, property, and a disciplined, organized plan to get from A to B.

The family frowned on those who didn't plan for tomorrow or who squandered their future on good times. A good plan, they often said, considers everything, especially those things holding you back from accomplishing what you want to achieve. Our elders realized that everything in nature runs according to an orderly master plan. They left little to luck or chance. They understood that while freedom—and even chaos—exists in nature, nevertheless, it is governed by natural laws.

There is no freedom without organization. I will develop a master plan for my future.

THE PRICE OF THE SOUL

It's about looking at the Amos and Andy in all of us and what we've had to do. By and large, as a people, we've had to be more like what white people want us to be to get over than we've been able to be who we are and express ourselves openly and honestly. So we sit with all these pent-up frustrations and undeclared feelings. . . .

We're in a struggle for the soul of this country. We're in a struggle for America's moral center. And unless that can be made straight, I'm not too sure any of the other battles are winnable.

—Harry Belafonte,[5] 1993

REFLECTION: Authors George Davis and Glegg Watson gave the Faustian concept of a man selling his soul for false prosperity a novel twist in their 1982 landmark book, *Black Life in Corporate America*, when they discussed the exorbitant price that many African Americans pay to enter the white corporate world. Only the strong and secure in soul and spirit manage to make it work for them. Davis and Watson interviewed Black corporate maven Jack Dockett about what internal changes are required to survive corporate life.

"Most of them [African Americans] don't know and don't care much about Black culture or any other kind of culture," Dockett explained. "They just want to make that money. They talk that talk just like the white guys. They have no racial consciousness at all."

This is the moral compromise to which Belafonte refers. Nothing is more valuable than your soul, your integrity, your sense of self. Guard and protect those parts of yourself with all your might. No job or amount of money is worth staying in a situation where you are not respected or valued.

Nothing is worth my soul or my integrity.

BLACK PRESS

I know that there are many papers in the country whose editors make great profession of love for colored citizens; but they are partisan advocates, striving for partisan advantage, and have no more real, practical love for the Negro than the editors of newspapers, avowedly their enemies. I have more respect for the latter than for the former. An open enemy is an easier man to handle than a hypocritical friend. A man who preaches one thing and practices another, is beneath contempt. . . . Let those ignorant Negroes, who pretend that they can not understand why colored newspapers are published, answer this question; and if they can not, let them slink away out of the sight of honest men who understand the serious nature of the Negro problem, and are honestly endeavoring to solve it in the right way. . . .

. . . How are we to overcome this tremendous influence? Can we reasonably expect other men to use their lungs to cry out for us when we are wronged and outraged and robbed and murdered? If we do, let us look at the white papers of the South and learn from them the necessary lesson, that the only way we can hope ever to win our fight is to arm ourselves as our opponents do, support those newspapers alone that support us, and support those men alone who support us.

—T. Thomas Fortune,[6] 1880

REFLECTION: For many decades, African Americans saw themselves represented in a white press in images designed to startle, shock, and disgust. In 1847, Black abolitionist Frederick Douglass raised funds to buy a printing press and start his own newspaper, *North Star*, after realizing that white publications were not accurately reporting the slavery question. When he was asked "Why publish a Negro newspaper?" Douglass replied: "I still see before me a life of toil and trials. But justice must be done, the truth must be told. I will not be silent." With Black firebrand Martin R. Delany as co-editor, *North Star* explained the oppression of our people in a way that no other publication could, gaining more support for the abolitionist cause.

In the tradition of Douglass's newspaper, African American newspapers have been in the forefront of the struggle for equality throughout the years. Instead of asking why they exist, we should praise the long list of newspapers that have articulated our struggle. We need their voices, their presence.

I will honor and support the African American press. The Black press is a powerful tool for our freedom.

Part 14

STRATEGIES FOR CHANGE

THE REVOLUTION

In fine, the nation presumes upon the citizenship of the Negro but is oblivious to the fact that it must confer citizenship before it can expect reciprocity. Until twenty million people are completely interwoven into the fabric of our society they are under no obligation to behave as if they were.

What I am saying is that whether we like the word or not, the condition of our people dictates what can only be called revolutionary attitudes. It is no longer acceptable to allow racists to define Negro manhood—and it will have to come to pass that they can no longer define his weaponry. . . .

The acceptance of our present condition is the only form of extremism which discredits us before our children.

—Lorraine Hansberry,[1] 1962

REFLECTION: As the oppression of Black people escalates once again, the word "revolution" is in the air. But the new revolution demands more than just a clenched fist or a fashionable slogan. It demands a fundamental change on the part of each and every one of us. The new revolution must start within—in how we think, how we feel, how we act. The new revolutionary attitude requires a deep reappraisal of our lives, our goals, and our commitment to the larger world outside ourselves.

Both Malcolm X and Martin Luther King, Jr., often spoke of the search for truth as the foundation of our struggle. Now is the time for us to search our souls and truly come to know ourselves. For revolution no longer depends on the violent overthrow of the "powers that be." Instead, we must commit to overthrowing everything inside of us that blocks us from full participation in the future of this nation.

The first step to real revolution starts with me.

CHANGE

Man cannot hold back the tide of change; we cannot experience the drastic transformations that have taken place in our physical world which are affecting our means of communication and transportation and still maintain an absolute status quo in our society. The unfortunate thing is that man exalts change in almost everything but himself. We have moved centuries ahead in inventing a new world in which to live, but we know little or nothing about our own role in this changing world, how to adjust morally and spiritually, how to accommodate. And so there is a strong effort on the part of many in this country to maintain obsolete customs and mores, traditions of an outmoded society in this new world in which we find ourselves—trying, as someone once said, to continue putting new wines in old skins and new patches on old garments.

—John Conyers, Jr.,[2] 1969

REFLECTION: Some of the more conservative members of our people say that blackness as a bargaining chip is played out. They believe it's a part of the old status quo that's holding us back, and it must go. The only way to appeal to America, they insist, is with an emphasis on merit and morality. They say that race no longer sets limits on African American life as it once did.

There is some truth to all of this. And yet, after years of adverse socialization and conditioning, many of us don't really comprehend all the options open to us now. Many of us remain locked into the narrow horizons of oppression because of powerful psychological and social chains. These issues must be addressed before we can accept our complete humanity. Change is difficult when our heads are full of self-doubt, anger, and shame. We actualize our lives when we no longer allow our doubts to control and limit us.

I must examine and discard any obsolete behaviors so I can be free to meet new challenges.

PEOPLE BEFORE PROFITS

"People before profits" means that we will do whatever is necessary to wipe out, at long last, the poisons of racism and sexism that divide our people while bringing profits and power to our enemies. . . .

"People before profits" means that we will reconstruct and expand our collapsing social services, giving every child the right to creative, bilingual, bicultural education, every young person the right to a secure and productive future, every mother the right to economic independence and every senior the right to a healthy and happy retirement.

—Angela Davis,[3] 1980

REFLECTION: Picture a world where the love of profit would not deny good health care to anyone. Picture a world where the love of profit would not refuse children of all races a good education. Where profits before people would not mandate the abandonment of the elderly and the disabled. Where profits before people would not entice companies to exploit workers. Where greed would not lead to the oppression of women for cheap commercialism. Where greed would not sanction the rape of our precious earth.

When you spend your money, make sure you know where your dollars are going. Do not invest in or buy products from companies that worship at the altar of profits with no concern for the well-being of people and our planet.

Greed destroys all of us. I pledge to create a world where people are as important as profits.

THE MAINSTREAM

The Negro must move, and will move, in the mainstream of American life. The American dream is the just and lawful heritage of Negro Americans, who have labored and died to defend their country and to help the economic, educational, and cultural life that makes it great. It is not through the withdrawal of any group, but through the fervent, united efforts of decent people of good will of every race, color, and creed that the system can be made to work for the benefit of all men.

The true worth of any nation is determined by that nation's treatment of its most disadvantaged citizens. It is determined also by its success or failure to honor its own bond, which, for the United States of America, is nothing less than total freedom of opportunity for every citizen. It is a bond long overdue American Negroes, and today, the American credo faces its gravest challenge. How this challenge is met will not be measured in terms of the gross national product or progress to the moon, but in terms of national morality.

—Whitney M. Young, Jr.,[4] 1969

REFLECTION: Moving into the mainstream has always been a hazardous proposition for Blacks. When a Black person enters an integrated work situation, that opportunity weighs heavily on the new employee. If the worker does well, "he's not like the rest of them." If the worker does poorly, "she's just like all the rest of them!" If a white worker fails, the entire white race is not indicted for his or her individual failure.

The situation will only improve if we refuse to be deterred by locked doors. When one brave pioneer falls, another must stand ready to take his place. A Black employee must recover from any setback, analyze his or her errors, and get back into the race.

"I don't want to work with white folks," a co-worker commented recently. "It's not worth the trouble." But it is worth the trouble, because individual excellence on the job goes far beyond our own personal achievements. Each of us is laying the groundwork for those who will come after us. Other Americans have climbed this rocky path to opportunity and we must do so as well.

Failure to persevere is the biggest foe of progress. To go forward in life, to move into the mainstream—I cannot falter or concede.

BLACK DOLLAR POWER

Wherever you spend your money is where you create a job. If you live in Harlem, and you spend your money in Chicago, you create jobs for people in Chicago. If you are Black and the businesses are run by people who are not Black, then the people who are not Black come in at 9 a.m.; leave at 5 p.m. and take the wealth to the communities in which they live.

—Tony Brown,[5] 1985

REFLECTION: Many African Americans have understood the potential of Black spending power for decades. When Martin Luther King, Jr., wanted to drive home his point about desegregating public transportation in Montgomery, Alabama, he worked out a plan to keep Black people off the buses. This tactic forced local whites to the bargaining table. Decreased revenue produced an immediate moral transformation that had not been possible to legislate.

The same tactic was used in Harlem in the late 1940s when Blacks picketed and boycotted white merchants who were selling them inferior goods at inflated prices and treating them rudely. An agreement was reached when the boycott hit white store owners in the cash register.

Never underestimate the spending power of your African American dollar in creating social change. Our communities are our strength! Wisely spending our dollars guarantees that they remain strong and become even stronger.

I will think before I spend. I will patronize those who support my community. I will make every dollar count!

KEEPING THE DOORS OPEN

The position of the Negro today in America is the tragic but inevitable consequence of centuries of unequal treatment. Measured by any benchmark of comfort or achievement, meaningful equality remains a distant dream for the Negro. . . . It is because of the legacy of unequal treatment that we now must permit the institutions of this society to give consideration to race in making decisions about who will hold the positions of influence, affluence and prestige in America. For far too long, the doors to those positions have been shut to Negroes. If we are ever to become a fully integrated society, one in which the color of a person's skin will not determine the opportunities available to him or her, we must be willing to take steps to open those doors. I do not believe that anyone can truly look into America's past and still find that a remedy for the effects of that past is impermissible.

—Justice Thurgood Marshall,[6] *1979*

REFLECTION: In America today, there should be no need for set-asides and quotas. However, this is not an equal opportunity nation, and discrimination still exists. A woman interviewed on a television news program said: "If you're hiring people for a job and you've got a tough choice, you hire the one who looks like you, that talks like you. That way you're not getting an unknown commodity."

This kind of thinking is what prompted the marches and picketing of the 1960s. The men at the firehouse don't want a woman there. The privileged traders at the brokerage houses don't want a Black or Hispanic there. But blame doesn't solve anything. Let's find a way to redress the inequalities and establish a new balance. If the current remedies aren't working, then we must find new ones that will.

To find a remedy for a wrong, I must first admit there is a problem. Today, I will take steps to open new doors for myself and my race.

VIGILANCE

Vigil . . . implies watchfulness. Anyone trying to obtain perfection is faced with various obstacles in life which tend to sidetrack him. Here, therefore, I mean watchfulness against elements that might be destructive from within and without. I don't try to set standards of perfection for anyone else. I do feel everyone does try to reach his better self, his full potential, and what that consists of depends on each individual. Whatever the goal is, moving toward it does require vigilance.

—*John Coltrane,*[7] *1965*

REFLECTION: Life is full of distractions that can sidetrack us from our goals. Temptations lurk everywhere to divert us from our chosen path.

Our biggest battle is inside ourselves, struggling with those self-defeating tendencies in our own character. You know you have a hard day at the job tomorrow but you decide to stay out late. You put off doing your projects until the last minute and wonder why they're not up to par. You promise to discuss an important problem with your mate after dinner, but you schedule a late-day business meeting that's certain to sap your strength. What's going on here?

We must learn to remain vigilant at all times. We must plan our time carefully and stick to our agenda. If we fail, we must not blame others. Everything that goes wrong in our lives is not the fault of an oppressive system. Now is the time to be vigilant and ever watchful of detours that can guarantee disaster.

I will be vigilant in all of my daily choices and actions. Nothing will deter me from getting what is rightfully mine.

THE GOOD LIFE

The twofold challenge that confronts us means we do not have time to waste . . . soaking up the trappings of an affluent society. We need to have a serious outlook most of the time, both on and off the job.

What is needed is a great deal of intellectual honesty, which can only be born of knowledge, awareness, and information about what is going on in the larger world around us, as well as what is going on in our immediate communities, which are a part of that larger world and yet are a part from it. We need to keep on learning, reading, and discussing. In general, we need to take a serious view of the world in which we live.

—H. Naylor Fitzhugh,[8] 1974

REFLECTION: Some among us act as though our job is done and our mission is accomplished. Our college degrees and creature comforts have made us complacent, sated, and oblivious to the fact that our struggle still continues.

We get so caught up in our tenuous achievements and in living the "good life" that our spiritual connection to the bigger agendas of our community has become imperiled. The bloat of our existence has deadened our souls. The numbing and the isolation that the safe haven of materialism breeds has crept up on us unnoticed.

To truly take part in this life, we must be in the world and approach each day with a zest for learning from both old and new experiences. We must be eager to participate in every way possible. We must get serious about the business of living. There is no time to waste.

I will not be sidetracked from life's important challenges by things that don't matter. We grow, learn, and progress by our focused determination and willingness to stay serious.

AWARE AND ALERT

The Negro in his present plight, however, does not see possibilities until it is too late. He exercises too much "hindsight," and for that reason he loses ground in the hotly contested battles of life. The Negro as a rule waits until a thing happens before he tries to avert it. He is too much like a man whom the author once saw knocked down in a physical combat. Instead of dodging the blow when it was being dealt he arose from his prostration dodging it.

—Carter G. Woodson,[9] 1933

REFLECTION: At times it seems we're being hit with one blow after another. We think we've been blindsided, and we ask ourselves, How did that happen? Where did that come from? The truth of the matter is that we saw it coming all along, but we were too slow to respond.

We continued working long hours for a promotion even though the boss hinted at a wage freeze. We continued driving the car even though the brakes were acting up. We ignored our lover's sadness and silence, and yet we were shocked and wounded when we discovered the infidelity. We knew corporations were giving less support for affirmative action, but we were stunned by the Republican sweep.

If we take a hard look at how these so-called surprises first entered our lives, we'll realize that we were usually forewarned. But we were too numbed by the overwhelming flood of daily incidents to heed the warning signs. Now we have to wake up and break through our numbness. We can no longer afford to react mindlessly to the ceaseless march of events.

I must learn to anticipate the blow before it lands. I will strive to remain awake and alert instead of going back to sleep.

THE CROSSROADS

The Black people of the world have, therefore, come at last to destiny's crossroads. They must make some fundamental decisions as a single people. The one hopeful sign is that they are slowly and painfully coming to their hitherto beclouded senses, coming to realize that they are one people with a common destiny and that, no matter how scattered over the world, the treatment suffered by one Black group is suffered by all. But there is a terrible crisis of leadership at the crossroads. There is no united leadership group or any real effort to create one. The great difficulty is that Black leaders . . . do not know what their own heritage is. They are almost wholly ignorant of their own cultural source from which independent, original thinking springs and progress is inspired.

—Chancellor Williams,[10] 1974

REFLECTION: In recent decades, many financially secure African Americans have stuck their heads in the sand, saying: "I don't want any part of this Black thing." Many of our leaders have fallen silent and inactive, and without creative leadership, there cannot be any workable solutions for the tidal wave of challenges battering our community. To overcome our problems, we must rethink our old approaches and strategies. Our destiny depends on our ability to create wholly original solutions for all Black people. To do this, we must rely on our heritage, our strength, our creativity, and our faith in the Creator. We cannot afford to submit or surrender. We are at the crossroads of our destiny.

Every obstacle must strengthen my will to lead my people beyond the crossroads.

THE TWENTY-FIRST CENTURY

Wherever we are on the face of this earth, we are an African people. We have got to understand that any problem faced by Africans is the collective problem of all the African people in the world, and not just the problem of the Africans who live in any one part of the world. . . .

In the twenty-first century there are going to be a billion African people on this earth. We have to ask ourselves, "Are we ready for the twenty-first century?" Do we go into the twenty-first century begging and pleading or insisting and demanding? We have to ask and answer that question and we have to decide if we are going to be the rearguard for somebody else's way of life, or do we rebuild our own way of life, or will we be the vanguard to rebuild our own nation.

—John Henrik Clarke,[11] 1991

REFLECTION: Dr. Clarke's question is the most important one confronting African Americans today: "Are we ready for the twenty-first century?" The current answer is a resounding NO! We must move past the petty quarrels over strategy, past old defeats and victories, to focus on the challenges of the technological age ahead. We must arm ourselves with an education that will prepare us for any manner of change.

Preparation for tomorrow requires planning today. Without education, our people will be battling for status in our society with our hands tied behind our backs. We must elevate our vision if we are to claim a place in tomorrow's world. We must choose whether we're going to let others decide our future for us or take the future in our own hands and decide matters for ourselves.

Will I be prepared for life in the twenty-first century? Am I learning what will be required to compete tomorrow?

LEADERSHIP

He is an expression or symbol, if you will, of the best traits of his people. There is a sure sense of dignity about him and his very physical strength bespeaks something of the restlessness and courage which characterized the bulk of the vilified black men of the period—a people conditioned by the terrors of ruthless oppression and communicating their spirit from generation to generation; not by precept but by example—now graphic, now more or less obscure; now passive, now insurrectionary, but always passed on . . . in a word, one senses that here is a man!

—Theodore Ward,[12] *1945*

REFLECTION: Leadership is not the easiest life path to follow at a time when tabloid journalism seeks to topple every person who rises above mediocrity. This has been especially true of the media's presentation of our greatest African American leaders from Paul Robeson to Malcolm X to Thurgood Marshall. When Spike Lee's film *Malcolm X* opened in November 1992, newspapers quickly challenged Malcolm's leadership credentials by saying only one in four young Blacks knew anything about the Black leader.

Leadership can't be manufactured, promoted, or sold. Leadership resides in the words and deeds of the leaders that inspire us to move from paralysis to positive action.

We must guard the memories and the accomplishments of those who have dared to take on the mantle of leadership. We must bring the inspiring qualities of our greatest leaders to bear on our own lives. Each of us can emulate the unmistakable qualities of true leadership every day.

I will discover and empower the leader that sleeps within me.

POSITIVE THINKING

Many people have a tendency to look at life negatively instead of positively, but I think the negative is there only to accentuate the positive, like a test. All of us have endured tribulations, but to let that embitter us doesn't make any sense. Negative things seem to work on the person who has the negative feelings, more than on the persons or conditions you feel negative about. You become the victim. When things were rough for me, I didn't want to victimize myself twice by thinking negatively.

If I get a couple of trees, and if I don't prune those trees, one tree will grow over the other and stunt the growth of the other. So I have to clear it out. I have to allow it to grow and breathe. That tree has to breathe. We're the same way. . . . No one is innocent of not having a few weaknesses, like negative thinking. If we can clear those weaknesses away, we can allow our strength to grow.

You can get up in the morning and feel bad, that happens. But try to think of something positive, and that will kind of brighten up the day a little bit. They say faith can move mountains. Well, I believe it.

—McCoy Tyner,[13] 1975

REFLECTION: No doubt you have met people whose entire outlook is one of doom and gloom. Their every word reeks of negativity and pessimism. In McCoy Tyner's terms, they see themselves as victims of life. The odds are stacked against them. Every setback imaginable lurks just outside their front door.

Playing the role of victim removes the burden of responsibility from their lives. It's everybody else's fault that their lives are as they are. For them, being victims makes it okay to indulge in the full range of crippled emotions.

When we invest in negativity, we invest in maintaining our role as victims. When we invest in the positive, we invest in the promise of unlimited potential.

It is our hopes, our dreams, our positive outlook that has always kept us moving forward through the eye of the storm. This way of thinking energizes us and nourishes our growth. Steer clear of those with bleak outlooks. Keep pace with those who look forward, not back or down.

There is no room for negativity in my life. I see the positive possibilities in all things.

COMMITMENTS

Until we are determined to change the condition of things, and raise ourselves above the position in which we are now prostrated, we must hang our heads in sorrow, and hide our faces in shame. It is enough to know that these things are so; the causes we care little about. Those we have been examining, complaining about, and moralising over, all our life time. This we are weary of. What we desire to learn now is, how to effect a remedy; this we have endeavored to point out. Our elevation must be the result of self-efforts, and work of our own hands. No other human power can accomplish it. If we but determine it shall be so, it will be so.

—Martin R. Delany,[14] 1852

REFLECTION: How many times have you failed to keep a commitment? How many times have you broken a promise? We've all done these things. We promise to call or to return something we borrowed and then never follow through. We make long apologies and vow that it will never happen again. Until the next time.

Before reneging on a promise, we must think of the consequences for ourselves and others. When we're responsible and reliable, we feel good about ourselves. Every time we fulfill a commitment or promise, we gain that much more respect in the eyes of others. With each goal-directed action, we take more control of our lives and determine our future. A consistent failure to be dependable brings shame to us as individuals and dishonor to our race.

We must deliver on our promises. Keeping our commitments is the only way to change our conditions.

REGENERATION

It has been said that there is but one way to make a people great—it is an appeal to the people themselves; that all great regenerations are the universal movements of the mass. It has also been said that all great regenerations seem to have been the work of the few and tacitly accepted by the multitude. Both of these sayings seem to be right, for it takes the second to make the first. Observe that throughout the whole world a great revolution has begun. The darkness of centuries has been broken: the knowledge which made certain men seem as demi-gods in the past has been made widespread; a power more subtle than brute force and mightier than armed men is at work; men in general have begun to think—to recognize the royalty of the mind. That same power is everywhere abroad—it speaks, it conquers, it unites all.

—Mary McLeod Bethune,[15] 1937

REFLECTION: In our struggle for equality, the power of the mind has served us well. But we now seem stymied by the knowledge-worker economy and the world of cyberspace. As the options available to many of us begin to shrink, we continue to wait for the benevolence of others, only to find that it is not forthcoming. We have become a reactive people; we no longer initiate. We have some of the most gifted minds in the world in our ranks, but we refuse to employ them to our advantage. Instead, we keep looking to the same people, the same speeches, the same means, to address our concerns. Rather than emerging with new answers, we're giving up and saying that the battle might be lost for some of us.

We must regenerate. We must renew ourselves. We must come forth with a new plan for the new millennium. Think of the relief we'll feel when we finally discard our outmoded ideas and call on some of our newer faces to lead and inspire us. The rest of the world is on the move. We must be as well.

The regeneration of a people begins one person at a time, slowly gathering force until the few become the many.

NOTES

1. POWER AND POLITICS

1. P. B. S. Pinchback, legislator and African American Reconstruction leader of Louisiana, from a speech given in Cincinnati in 1875. Source: Herbert Aptheker, ed., *A Documentary History of the Negro People in the United States*, vol. 2 (New York: Citadel Press, 1979), 643.

2. John Henrik Clarke, writer and historian. Source: John H. Clarke, "The Growth of Racism in the West," *Black World*, October 1970, 10.

3. Rosa Parks, whose defiance on an Alabama bus started the modern Civil Rights Movement in 1955. Source: Rosa Parks with Gregory J. Reed, *Quiet Strength: The Faith, the Hope, and the Heart of a Woman Who Changed a Nation* (Grand Rapids, Mich.: Zondervan Publishing House, 1994), 23–24.

4. Bishop Turner, writer and activist, from a speech given in 1896. Source: Herbert Aptheker, ed., *A Documentary History of the Negro People in the United States*, vol. 2 (New York: Citadel Press, 1979), 757.

5. Edward Everett Brown, lawyer, from a speech given in 1888. *The Record: The Black Experience in America: 1619–1979* (New York: National Association for the Advancement of Colored People, 1981), 9.

6. William Pickens, writer and NAACP official, from a 1925 article. Source: Herbert Aptheker, ed., *A Documentary History of the Negro People in the United States*, vol. 3 (New York: Citadel Press, 1979), 86.

7. Marcus Garvey, nationalist leader, from an article originally published in *Negro World* (October 8, 1921). Source: *Encore*, November 19, 1979, 47.

8. Frances Ellen Watkins Harper, writer and activist, from a 1891 speech. Source: Gerda Lerner, ed., *Black Women in White America* (New York: Vintage, 1972), 194.

9. Camille Cosby, activist and wife of entertainer Bill Cosby. Source: Stephanie S. Oliver, "Camille Cosby: An Intimate Portrait," *Essence*, December 1989, 11.

10. C. T. Vivian, civil rights leader. Source: Studs Terkel, *Race* (New York: The New Press, 1992), 343.

11. Martin R. Delany, writer and publisher, from an 1852 article. Source: Howard Brotz, ed., *Negro Social and Political Thought: 1850–1920* (New York: Basic Books, 1966), 39.

2. CREATIVITY AND CULTURE

1. Randy Weston, jazz pianist. Source: "African-Rooted Rhythms," *Downbeat*, September 6, 1979, 19.

2. Oscar Brown, Jr., singer. Source: "Oscar Brown Jr.: Movin' On," *Impressions*, June 1976, 25.

3. Miles Davis, jazz trumpeter. Source: Miles Davis with Quincy Troupe, *Miles: The Autobiography* (New York: Simon & Schuster, 1989), 405–406.

4. Bill Gunn, writer and filmmaker. Source: "Bill Gunn: We Should Burn all the Books and Start all over Again," *Encore*, June 1973, 55.

5. Woodie King, playwright. Source: "Searching for Brothers Kindred: Rhythms & Blues of the 1950s," *Black Scholar*, November 1974, 20.

6. Ossie Davis, actor. Source: John Henrik Clarke, ed., *Harlem USA* (New York: Collier, 1971), 153–154.

7. Romare Bearden, artist, from an article originally published in 1934. Source: David L. Lewis, ed., *The Portable Harlem Renaissance Reader* (New York: Viking, 1994), 141.

8. Toni Morrison, Nobel Prize–winning writer. Source: Henry Louis Gates, Jr., and K. A. Appiah, eds., *Toni Morrison: Critical Perspectives Past and Present* (New York: Amistad Press, 1993), 374.

9. Jacob Lawrence, artist. Source: "Clarence Major Interviews Jacob Lawrence: The Expressionist," *Black Scholar*, November 1977, 19.

10. Elizabeth Catlett, artist. Source: "The Role of the Artist," *Black Scholar*, June 1978, 122.

11. Alexander Crummell, minister and advocate, from an 1898 article. Source: Leslie Fishel and Benjamin Quarles, eds., *The Black American* (Glenview, Ill.: Scott, Foresman, 1970), 355.

12. Jean Toomer, writer. Source: Darwin T. Turner, ed., *The Wayward and the Seeking* (Washington, D.C.: Howard University Press, 1980), 19.

3. SELF-ESTEEM

1. The Honorable Elijah Muhammad, former leader of the Nation of Islam. Source: Elijah Muhammad, *Message to the Blackman in America* (Chicago, Ill.: Mosque of Islam No. 2, 1965), 34.

2. Paul Robeson, activist and entertainer. Source: Paul Robeson, *Here I Stand* (Boston: Beacon, 1958), 100–101.

3. James Weldon Johnson, writer and diplomat. Source: James Weldon Johnson, *The Autobiography of an Ex-Colored Man* (1922; reprint, New York: Hill and Wang, 1960), 18.

4. John Edgar Wideman, writer. Source: John E. Wideman, *Brothers and Keepers* (London: Allison and Busby, 1985), 221.

5. Barbara Jordan, U.S. congresswoman. Source: Barbara Jordan and Shelby Hearon, *Barbara Jordan: A Self-Portrait* (New York: Doubleday, 1970), 62.

6. Booker T. Washington, educator and African American leader. Source: Howard Brotz, ed., *Negro Social and Political Thought: 1850–1920* (New York: Basic Books, 1966), 285.

7. Marcus Garvey, nationalist leader. Source: Amy-Jacques Garvey, ed., *Philosophy and Opinions of Marcus Garvey* (New York: Atheneum, 1970), 71.

8. Fannie Lou Hamer, Mississippi civil rights activist. Source: Garland Phyl, "Builders of a New South," *Ebony,* August 1966, 34–36.

9. Sammy Davis, Jr. Source: Sammy Davis Jr., Jane Boyar, and Burt Boyar, *Why Me?* (New York: Farrar Straus Giroux, 1989), 35–36.

10. Zora Neale Hurston, folklorist and writer. Source: Zora Neale Hurston, *Dust Tracks on a Road* (reprint, New York: Lippincott, 1971), 215.

11. Ralph Ellison, writer. Source: Ralph Ellison, *Shadow and Act* (New York: Random House, 1964), 112–113.

12. Dorothy West, writer. Source: Dorothy West, *The Richer, the Poorer* (New York: Doubleday, 1995), 171.

4. VALUES

1. Booker T. Washington, educator and African American leader. Source: Herbert Aptheker, ed., *A Documentary History of the Negro People in the United States,* vol. 3 (New York: Citadel Press, 1979), 754–755.

2. Frank Morgan, jazz saxophonist. Source: Ben Sidran, *Talking Jazz* (San Francisco: Pomegrante Books, 1992), 28.

3. Muhammad Ali, boxing champion. Source: Thomas Hauser, *Muhammad Ali: His Life and Times* (New York: Simon & Schuster, 1991), 189.

4. James Forman, civil rights activist. Source: James Forman, *The Making of Black Revolutionaries* (New York: Macmillian, 1972), 107.

5. Marian Wright Edelman, head of the Children's Defense Fund. Source: "An Agenda for Empowerment," *Essence*, May 1988, 133.

6. Chester Himes, writer. Source: Chester Himes, *Black on Black* (Garden City, N.Y.: Doubleday, 1973), 228–229.

7. Duke Ellington, jazz composer and bandleader. Source: Duke Ellington, *Music Is My Mistress* (Garden City, N.Y.: Doubleday, 1973), 259.

8. Dr. Alvin Poussaint, writer and educator. Source: "A Dialogue on Separatism," *Ebony*, August 1970, 68.

9. A. G. Gaston, businessman. Source: "How to Make a Million," *Ebony*, November 1975, 60.

10. Zora Neale Hurston, folklorist and writer. Source: Zora Neale Hurston, *Dust Tracks on a Road* (reprint, New York: Lippincott, 1971), 41.

11. William Strickland, writer. Source: "The Road since Brown: The Americanization of the Race," *Black Scholar*, September–October 1979, 8.

12. A. Elizabeth Delany, historian and writer. Source: Sarah Delany and A. Elizabeth Delany, *Having Our Say* (New York: Dell, 1994), 161–162.

13. Helen Howard, writer and activist, from a 1965 article.

Source: Gerda Lerner, ed., *Black Women in White America* (New York: Vintage, 1972), 311–313.

14. John H. Johnson, publisher. Source: John H. Johnson, *Succeeding Against the Odds* (New York: Amistad Press, 1992), 89–90.

15. Dick Gregory, comedian and activist. Source: Dick Gregory with Robert Lipsyte, *Nigger* (New York: Pocket Books, 1965), 25.

5. YOUTH

1. H. Claude Hudson, businessman and civil rights advocate. Source: Stanton L. Wormley and Lewis Fenderson, eds., *Many Shades of Black* (New York: William Morrow, 1969), 133.

2. Louis Armstrong, jazz trumpeter. Source: Stanton L. Wormley and Lewis Fenderson, eds., *Many Shades of Black* (New York: William Morrow, 1969), 133.

3. Ralph Ellison, writer. Source: Ralph Ellison, *Going to the Territory* (New York: Random House, 1986), 68, 74.

4. Ralph Abernathy, civil rights leader. Source: Ralph Abernathy, *And the Walls Came Tumbling Down* (New York: Harper & Row, 1989), 587.

5. Matilda, writer of this 1827 letter. Source: Herbert Aptheker, ed., *A Documentary History of the Negro People in the United States*, vol. 1. (New York: Citadel Press, 1979), 89.

6. Samuel Proctor, writer and former Peace Corps official. Source: Samuel D. Proctor, *The Young Negro in America: 1960–1980* (New York: Association Press, 1966), 55.

7. Kweisi Mfume, U.S. congressman. Source: Herb Boyd

and Robert L. Allen, eds., *Brotherman: The Odyssey of Black Men in America* (New York: One World/Ballantine, 1995), 825.

8. H. Rap Brown, 1960s activist. Source: H. Rap Brown, *Die Nigger Die* (New York: Dial Press, 1969), 18–19.

9. Malcolm X, nationalist leader, from a 1964 speech. Source: George Breitman, ed., *Malcolm X Speaks* (New York: Grove Press, 1966), 136.

6. EDUCATION

1. James Baldwin, writer, from a 1980 article. Source: James Baldwin, *The Price of the Ticket* (New York: St. Martin's Press, 1985), 657–658.

2. Arthur A. Schomburg, historian and archivist. Source: Alain Locke, ed., *The New Negro* (1925; reprint, New York: Atheneum, 1970), 231.

3. Carl T. Rowan, columnist and journalist. Source: "Hair Ain't Where It's At," *Encore*, October 1973, 38.

4. Marva Collins, educator. Source: Marva Collins and Civia Tamarkin, *Marva Collins' Way* (New York: G. P. Putnam's Sons, 1990), 21–22.

5. Dr. Fletcher Robinson, educator and family advocate. Source: *Black Books Bulletin*, fall 1977, 31.

6. Rose Smith, maternal grandmother of Robert Fleming. Source: Robert Fleming, "The Ritual of Survival," in *UpSouth*, ed. Malaika Adero (New York: The New Press, 1993), 39.

7. Samuel Cornish and John B. Russwurm, editors of the first African American newspaper, *Freedom's Journal* (1827). Source: Herbert Aptheker, ed., *A Documentary History of the*

Negro People in the United States, vol. 1 (New York: Citadel Press, 1979), 83.

8. Jitu Weusi, community activist. Source: "From Relevance to Excellence," *Black Books Bulletin,* spring–winter 1974, 22.

9. Jersey Joe Walcott, boxing champion. Source: Stanton L. Wormley and Lewis Fenderson, eds., *Many Shades of Black* (New York: William Morrow, 1969), 226.

7. FAMILY

1. Dr. Wade Nobles, authority on human relationships. Source: "The Black Family and Its Children," *Black Books Bulletin,* spring 1978, 12.

2. Alice Childress, writer. Source: "Negro Woman in Literature," *Freedomways* 6 (winter 1966): 19.

3. W. E. B. Du Bois, scholar, activist, and writer, from a 1912 editorial in *The Crisis.* Source: W. E. B. Du Bois, *An ABC of Color* (New York: International Publishers, 1964), 44.

4. June Jordan, poet and activist. Source: "Don't Talk about My Mama," *Essence,* December 1987, 126.

5. Sidney Poitier, actor. Source: Sidney Poitier, *This Life* (New York: Alfred A. Knopf, 1980), 369–370.

6. Alex Haley, journalist and author of the best-selling book *Roots.* Source: Interview, *Black Scholar,* September 1976, 39.

7. Adrienne Kennedy, playwright. Source: Adrienne Kennedy, *People Who Led to My Plays* (New York: Alfred A. Knopf, 1987), 12.

8. George Jackson, writer and activist. Source: George Jackson, *Soledad Brother: The Prison Letters of George Jackson* (New York: Bantam, 1970), 46.

8. COMMUNITY

1. Kwame Touré (Stokely Carmichael), educator and activist. Source: Floyd Barbour, ed., *The Black Power Revolt* (New York: Porter Sargent Publisher, 1968), 70.

2. Adam Clayton Powell, Jr., former U.S. congressman. Source: Adam Clayton Powell Jr., *Adam by Adam* (New York: Dial Press, 1971), 249–250.

3. W. E. B. Du Bois, scholar, activist, from a 1947 article. Source: "Can the Negro Expect Freedom by 1965?" *Encore*, November 19, 1979, 45.

4. Ray Charles, singer. Source: Ray Charles with David Ritz, *Brother Ray* (New York: DaCapo, 1992), 286.

5. Edward W. Brooke, former U.S. senator. Source: "Black Business, Problems, and Prospects," *Black Scholar*, April 1975, 2–3.

6. A. Phillip Randolph, labor leader and activist. Source: Interview, *Muhammad Speaks*, April 1, 1963, 3–4.

7. H. Rap Brown, 1960s activist. Source: H. Rap Brown, *Die Nigger Die* (New York: Dial Press, 1969), 38.

8. Whitney M. Young, Jr., civil rights activist. Source: "Crime—On and Off the Street," *Amsterdam News*, April 3, 1968, 20.

9. Andrew Billingsley, sociologist and educator. Source: Interview, "Our Backbone Is Black and Blue Collar," *Newsday*, February 4, 1993, 93.

10. Kwame Touré (Stokely Carmichael), educator and activist. Source: Mitchell Goodman, ed., *The Movement Toward a New America* (New York: Alfred A. Knopf, 1970), 180.

11. James O. Plinton, Jr., businessman. Source: Profile, *Encore*, October 1974, 26.

12. Lucille Clifton, poet and writer. Source: "We Are the Grapevine," *Essence*, May 1985, 129.

9. RELATIONSHIPS

1. Lena Horne, actress. Source: Lena Horne with Richard Schiekel, *Lena* (London: Andre Deutsch Ltd., 1966), 82.
2. Della Reese, entertainer. Source: "Della Reese Talks Frankly about the Burdens and Blessings of Family and Home," *Jet*, March 29, 1982, 58.
3. Pearl Bailey, actress and singer. Source: Pearl Bailey, *Talking to Myself* (New York: Pocket, 1973), 65.
4. Richard Pryor, comedian. Source: *Interview*, March 1986, 51.
5. Maulana Ron Karenga, educator and writer. Source: "In Love and Struggle: Toward a Greater Togetherness," *Black Scholar*, March 1975, 24–25.
6. Toni Cade Bambara, educator and writer. Source: Roseann P. Bell, Bettye J. Parker, and Beverly Guy-Sheftall, *Sturdy Black Bridges: Visions of Black Women in Literature* (New York: Anchor, 1979), 244–245.
7. Imamu Amiri Baraka, writer and activist. Source: Imanu Amiri Baraka, *Raise Race Rays Raze: Essays since 1965* (New York: Vintage, 1972), 153.
8. Myrlie Evers-Williams, civil rights activist. Source: "Remembering Medgar," *Essence*, February 1986, 60.

10. BLACK WOMEN AND BLACK MEN

1. Sojourner Truth, abolitionist and writer. Source: Gerda Lerner, ed., *Black Women in White America* (New York: Vintage, 1972), 570.

2. Elise Johnson McDougald, writer. Source: David L. Lewis, ed., *The Portable Harlem Renaissance Reader* (New York: Viking, 1994), 75.

3. Amy Garvey, editor and writer. Source: Interview, *Encore*, May 1973, 68.

4. James Van Der Zee, photographer. Source: James Van Der Zee, Owen Dodson, and Camille Billops, *The Harlem Book of the Dead* (Dobbs Ferry, N.Y.: Morgan & Morgan, 1978), 68.

5. John O. Killens, writer. Source: "The Black Culture Generation Gap," *Black World*, August 1973, 23.

6. Nathan Hare, writer and educator. Source: "Will the Real Black Man Please Stand Up?" *Black Scholar*, June 1971, 35.

7. Haki R. Madhubuti, poet and founder of Third World Press. Source: "A Call to Black Men," *Black Books Bulletin*, spring 1978–1980, 45.

8. Dorothy Dandridge, actress. Source: Dorothy Dandridge with Earl Conrad, *Everything and Nothing* (London: Abelard-Schuman Ltd., 1970), 207.

9. William H. Grier and Price M. Cobbs, psychiatrists. Source: William H. Grier and Price M. Cobbs, *Black Rage* (New York: Basic Books, 1968), 59.

11. A LIVING GOD

1. Henry McNeal Turner, minister and legislator, from a 1868 speech. Source: *The Record: The Black Experience in America 1619–1979*, (New York: National Association for the Advancement of Colored People, 1981), 6.

2. Annetta G. Jefferson, educator and playwright. Source:

"The Negro as the Conscience of America," *The Crisis*, February 1961, 70–71.

3. Dr. Howard Thurman, minister and educator. Source: "What Happened to Hell?" *Ebony*, February 1961, 48.

4. Ethel Waters, singer and actress. Source: Ethel Waters with Charles Samuels, *His Eye Is on the Sparrow* (Garden City, N.Y.: Doubleday, 1951), 93.

5. Ray Charles, singer. Source: Ray Charles with David Ritz, *Brother Ray* (New York: DaCapo, 1992), 296.

6. Richard Wright, writer. Source: Richard Wright, *12 Million Black Voices* (1941; reprint, New York: Thunder's Mouth Press, 1988), 130–31.

7. Dr. C. Eric Lincoln, theologian and educator. Source: Interview, *Black Books Bulletin*, spring 1976, 35.

8. Martin Luther King, Jr., minister and activist. Source: James M. Washington, ed., *A Testament of Hope: The Essential Writings of Martin Luther King, Jr.* (New York: Harper & Row, 1986), 40.

9. Benjamin E. Mays, theologian and educator. Source: Benjamin Mays, *The Negro's God* (1938; reprint, New York: Atheneum, 1968), 25.

10. Dr. Archibald J. Carey, Jr., minister. Source: "What Happened to Hell?" *Ebony*, February 1961, 48.

11. Roosevelt Sykes, bluesman. Source: Robert Neff and Anthony Connor, *Blues* (Boston: David R. Godine, 1975), 8.

12. RACE AND RACISM

1. Benjamin Banneker, mathematician and astronomer, from a 1791 letter to Thomas Jefferson. Source: Floyd

Barbour, ed., *The Black Power Revolt* (Boston: Porter Sargent Publishers, 1968), 18.

2. Frederick Douglass, abolitionist and writer. Source: Frederick Douglass, *Life and Times of Frederick Douglass* (1892; reprint, New York: Collier, 1962), 202.

3. Derrick Bell, writer and educator. Source: Derrick Bell, *Faces at the Bottom of the Well* (New York: Basic Books, 1992), 124.

4. Thurgood Marshall, former U.S. Supreme Court justice. Source: Interview, *Ebony*, November 1980, 222.

5. Mahalia Jackson, gospel singer. Source: Jules Schwerin, *Got to Tell It: Mahalia Jackson—Queen of Gospel* (New York: Oxford University Press, 1992), 110.

6. Gordon Parks, writer and photographer. Source: Gordon Parks, *Voices in the Mirror* (New York: Doubleday, 1970), 89–90.

7. Lerone Bennett, editor and writer. Source: Lerone Bennett and the editors of *Ebony*, *The White Problem in America* (Chicago: Johnson Publishing Co., 1966), 6.

8. Jackie Robinson, baseball pioneer. Source: Stanton L. Wormsley and Lewis Fenderson, eds., *Many Shades of Black* (New York: William Morrow, 1969), 216.

13. FREEDOM

1. Frederick Douglass, abolitionist and writer. Source: Frederick Douglass, *Life and Times of Frederick Douglass* (1892; reprint, New York: Collier, 1962), 661.

2. Dr. C. Eric Lincoln, theologian and educator. Source: C. Eric Lincoln, *Sounds of the Struggle* (New York: Apollo Editions, 1968), 27.

3. James Cone, theologian. Source: Interview, *Black Books Bulletin*, spring–winter 1976, 7.

4. Dizzy Gillespie, jazz trumpeter. Source: Art Taylor, *Notes and Tones* (New York: 1977), 138.

5. Harry Belafonte, entertainer and activist. Source: "The Political Is Personal," *New York Times*, September 9, 1993, sec. C, 6.

6. T. Thomas Fortune, editor and writer. Source: "The Afro-American Editor's Mission by Eminent Journalists: 1891," *Encore*, June 20, 1977, 28.

14. Strategies for Change

1. Lorraine Hansberry, writer and playwright, from an April 27, 1962, letter. Source: Lorraine Hansberry, adapted by Robert Nemiroff, *To Be Young, Gifted and Black* (New York: Signet, 1970), 221–222.

2. John Conyers, Jr., U.S. congressman. Source: Stanton L. Wormsley and Lewis Fenderson, eds., *Many Shades of Black* (New York: William Morrow, 1969), 6.

3. Angela Davis, writer and activist. "To Save Our Nation," *Freedomways* 20 (second quarter 1980): 86.

4. Whitney M. Young, Jr., civil rights activist. Source: Stanton L. Wormley and Lewis Fenderson, eds., *Many Shades of Black* (New York: William Morrow, 1969), 81.

5. Tony Brown, TV-show host. Source: "Words of the Week," *Jet*, November 11, 1985, 38.

6. Thurgood Marshall, former U.S. Supreme Court justice, from his dissent in the 1978 Bakke case. Source: *Encore*, November 19, 1979, 49.

7. John Coltrane, jazz saxophonist. Source: C. O. Simp-

kins, *Coltrane: A Biography* (New York: Herndon House Publishers, 1975), 187.

8. H. Naylor Fitzhugh, businessman. Source: Profile, *Encore,* October 1974, 27.

9. Carter G. Woodson, writer and editor. Source: Carter G. Woodson, *The Mis-education of the Negro* (1933; reprint, New York: AMS Press, 1972), 141.

10. Chancellor Williams, writer and scholar. Source: Chancellor Williams, *The Destruction of Black Civilization* (Chicago: Third World Press, 1974), 334.

11. John Henrik Clarke, writer and historian. Source: Herb Boyd and Robert L. Allen, eds., *Brotherman: The Odyssey of Black Men in America* (New York: One World/Ballantine, 1995), 696–697.

12. Theodore Ward, playwright, from his landmark play *Our Lan'* (1945). Source: Doris E. Abramson, *Negro Playwrights in the American Theatre 1925–1959* (New York: Columbia University Press, 1969), 121.

13. McCoy Tyner, jazz pianist. Source: "Savant of the Astral Latitudes," *Downbeat,* September 11, 1975, 13.

14. Martin R. Delaney, abolitionist and writer, from 1852 writings. Source: *Encore,* November 19, 1970, 44.

15. Mary McLeod Bethune, educator. Source: Mary McLeod Bethune, "A People's Regeneration," *Chicago Defender,* August 8, 1937.

PERMISSIONS ACKNOWLEDGMENTS

Grateful acknowledgment is made to the following for permission to reprint previously published material:

Larry Birnbaum: Excerpt from "Randy Weston: African-Rooted Rhythms," *Down Beat Magazine,* September 6, 1979. Copyright © 1979 by Larry Birnbaum. Reprinted by permission of the author.

The Black Scholar: Excerpts from: "The Black Scholar Interviews Alex Haley," September 1976; "The Role of the Black Artist" by Elizabeth Catlett, June 1975; "Will the Real Black Man Please Stand Up?" by Nathan Hare, June 1971; "Black Business, Problems and Prospects" by Edward W. Brooke, April 1975; "In Love and Struggle: Toward a Greater Togetherness" by Ron Karenga, March 1975; "Clarence Major Interviews: Jacob Lawrence, The Expressionist" by Jacob Lawrence, November 1977; "Searching for Brothers Kindred: Rhythm and Blues of the 1950's" by Woodie King, Jr., November 1974; "The Road Since Brown" by William Strickland, September–October 1975. Reprinted by permission of *The Black Scholar.*

Children's Defense Fund: Excerpt from *The Measure of Our Success: A Letter to My Children and Yours* by Marian Wright Edelman, Beacon Press, Boston, 1992. Reprinted by permission of Children's Defense Fund.

Lucille Clifton: Excerpt from "We Are the Grapevine" by Lucille Clifton, *Essence,* May 1985. Reprinted by permission of the author.

Down Beat Magazine: McCoy Turner quote excerpted from "Savant of the Astral Latitudes" by Lee Underwood, *Down Beat Magazine,* September 11, 1975. Reprinted courtesy of *Down Beat Magazine.*

AUTHOR INDEX

ABOUT THE AUTHOR

Robert Fleming, a freelance journalist, formerly worked as a reporter for the *New York Daily News*, earning several honors, including a New York Press Club award and a Revson Fellowship in 1990. His articles have appeared in publications including *Essence*, *Black Enterprise*, *U.S. News & World Report*, *Omni*, and *The New York Times*. His poetry and essays have appeared in *UpSouth* and *In Search of Color Everywhere: A Collection of African American Poetry*.